Decoding Wagner

Unlocking the Masters Series, No. 1

Series Editor
Robert Levine

Decoding Wagner

An Invitation to His World of Music Drama

Thomas May

AMADEUS
PRESS

The author and publisher express gratitude to Starling Lawrence and W.W. Norton for kind permission to reprint quotes from *Selected Letters of Richard Wagner*, translated by Stewart Spencer and edited by Barry Millington, and to Seattle Opera and San Francisco Opera for generously providing photos from their productions of Wagner.

Published in 2004 by

Amadeus Press, LLC
512 Newark Pompton Turnpike
Pompton Plains, New Jersey 07444, USA

Reprinted in 2005

For sales, please contact

NORTH AMERICA   UNITED KINGDOM AND EUROPE

AMADEUS PRESS, LLC   ROUNDHOUSE PUBLISHING LTD.
c/o Hal Leonard Corp.   Millstone, Limers Lane
7777 West Bluemound Road   Northam, North Devon EX39 2RG, UK
Milwaukee, Wisconsin 53213, USA Phone: 01237-474474
Phone: 800-637-2852   Fax: 01237-474774
Fax: 414-774-3259   E-mail: roundhouse.group@ukgateway.net

E-mail: orders@amadeuspress.com
Website: www.amadeuspress.com

Printed in Canada

Library of Congress Cataloging-in-Publication Data

May, Thomas (Thomas Robert)
Decoding Wagner : an invitation to his world of music drama / by Thomas May.—
1st paperback ed.
        p. cm. — (Unlocking the masters series ; no. 1)
    Includes bibliographical references and discography.
    ISBN 1-57467-097-2
        1. Wagner, Richard, 1813–1883 Operas. 2. Operas—Analysis, appreciation.
    I. Title. II. Series.

ML410.W13M25 2004
782.1'092—dc22
                                                              2004018846

To my parents,
for encouraging my love of the arts
and for their unwavering support

Traulich und treu ist's nur in der Tiefe:
falsch und feig ist, was dort oben sich freut!

(Only in the depths is it safe and true:
False and craven, all that rejoices above!)

—*Das Rheingold*

Contents

Preface and Acknowledgments

Our age is one in which commercial pressures have exaggerated the rift between entertainment values and artistic ones. Anyone committed to the latter and concerned with their eclipse—if not eventual erasure—has much to learn from the example of Richard Wagner. Yet Wagner remains suspended in a paradoxical position shared by few other artists. On the one hand, the entertainment side of our cultural equation—the part that thinks in sound bytes and sidebars, reducing everything in its path to consumable quanta of information—perpetuates the illusion that the Wagner phenomenon can be grasped through a few readymade clichés. On the other, it is precisely one of those clichés that tends to ward off those who would otherwise have a strong affinity for Wagner's art: the notion that Wagner is impossibly daunting, cumbersome, "heavy," even—despite having been so clearly assimilated into the culture—a "dangerous" influence after all these years. It's a wonderfully poetic irony that in 2004 the British Foundation for Motoring voted Wagner's single best-known excerpt, the "Ride of the Valkyries," as the number one tune to avoid playing in the car on account of its propensity to cause accidents. Add to this the reputation of Wagner's more reprehensible personal characteristics, and it's no wonder so many decide to opt out of a better acquaintance and stick with the clichés.

Wagner is, after all, dangerous—in the sense, that is, that matters, the sense of all truly challenging art. *Decoding Wagner: An Invitation to His World of Music Drama* aims to offer a sensible overview of his achievement. You may have yet to encounter his music dramas. Perhaps your only brush thus far has been to hear the "Ride of the Valkyries" on the car radio (free, it is hoped, of accidents or road rage). Or you may have been put off entirely by the negative publicity that, in one form or another, has attached itself to the composer for over a century and a half. On the other hand, you might even have attended a whole *Ring* cycle or experienced *Tristan* or *Parsifal,* but there's a gnawing sense that too much eluded you, beyond a memorable musical impression of floating or an ecstatic but temporary euphoria.

This book is intended as an introduction for those who would like to delve more fully into these works. It places each of Wagner's major operas in context and considers his art as the amalgam of drama and music that it was for its creator. Certain core themes will be found to emerge—tracing their evolution and transformation over Wagner's life is a source of continual fascination—yet the *uniqueness* of each work is of equal concern. This book makes no pretensions to any sort of conclusive thoroughness (any book that does so betrays a fundamental misapprehension of its subject). Nor does it investigate the myriad controversies associated with "Wagnerism": the role of philosophy in Wagner's work, his altering political stances, his voluminous writings on aesthetics, his anti-Semitism and ideological preoccupations, misogyny vs. protofeminism in the operas, performance traditions, reception and production history, and so on. It's hard to find a controversy *not* associated with Wagner, since—possibly more than that of any other artist of the past two centuries—his work represents a kind of artistic uncertainty principle: the very act of interpreting automatically introduces the perceptions of the interpreter. These have all been rehearsed elsewhere at delirious length by generations of experts and are merely mentioned as context here.

The spotlight is on the works themselves, on the common ground behind the music and the drama—and on the relevance this continues to hold for us. Musical analysis is not contained here, nor is yet another series of glorified plot summaries intended (such summaries, incidentally, can be found in a number of the reference titles suggested for further reading). In other words, this book attempts to address readers who are looking for something more than dime-a-dozen (often dumbed-down) operatic Baedekers but who might be intimidated by technical details of how the music works. The focus remains more closely on Wagner and his developing art, with specific illustrations from musical examples contained on the accompanying two CDs of excerpts. *Decoding Wagner* invites the reader to encounter a composer still shrouded in rumor and misunderstanding and, to this day, a polarizing icon. But the issues with which he grappled as an artist—most resoundingly, his vision for enlarging the possibilities of expression—likewise remain ours.

This book would not have come to light without the tireless inspiration of my editor Robert Levine. His gently prodding encouragement, restorative brand of humor, and generous confidence are what every writer dreams of. To have shared his own passionate knowledge of Wagner into the bargain has been a windfall. I also want to thank everyone at Amadeus Press involved in shepherding the book so effectively to completion, especially Joanna Dalin for her keen editorial eye, Carol Flannery, Caroline Howell, and my publisher John Cerullo.

Since relocating to Seattle, I have found my enthusiasm rekindled by the Seattle Opera, which has a justified reputation for its imaginative productions of Wagner. I'm grateful to my friends there, in particular to Tina Ryker and Jonathan Dean, and to Mary Langholz of the Seattle Symphony for her encouragement. Thanks also go to my friends at the

San Francisco Opera: Wolfgang Willaschek, Claire Myers, and Robert Cable.

A finer mentor than Tim Page couldn't be imagined: his initial encouragement of my writing quite simply changed my life, while his friendship has been invaluable. I am also deeply thankful to the San Francisco Symphony's Larry Rothe for providing so many opportunities.

Thanks to my family for all their tremendous support—especially to my sister Susan Romanosky for her creative suggestions. When I've needed to bounce ideas around or recharge my batteries, Pierre Ruhe and James Hatch have been true-hearted colleagues and friends. Silvana Tropea and Tanvir Ahmed provided valuable feedback. I've also been fortunate to have my morale boosted by my friends from the editorial brain trust at Amazon.com: in particular, Jason Verlinde, Kevin ("Kenlon") Cole, Marc Greilsamer, and Renata Sadunas.

Finally, it's impossible to experience and write about Wagner without absorbing the endless store of insights accumulated by generations of his interpreters: both performers and commentators. Their work continues to increase our understanding of his inexhaustible genius but, above all, to make it an experience to enjoy.

Introduction
What's All the Fuss?

For a long time, it had simmered beneath the surface. Finally, between 1848 and 1849, an impulse to violent revolution ignited and flashed through Europe. This was the period that saw the publication of *The Communist Manifesto,* as well as the last gasp of a longed-for democratic republic among progressive Germans (not to be made a reality until the ill-fated Weimar Republic in the century to come). Right in the thick of the action and its aftermath stood the ambitious composer Richard Wagner. So rash had his involvement been that, by his thirty-sixth birthday in May 1849, the weary and breathless revolutionary was on the lam from the authorities. With a warrant out for his arrest as one of the principal agitators in the Dresden phase of the uprising, he crossed the border into Switzerland's safe haven, thanks to a feigned identity and passport provided by his friend Franz Liszt. His lucky escape spared him imprisonment—and a possible death sentence. Wagner would remain an exile from his native land for a dozen years.

This has to stand out as one of the most colorful series of episodes in Wagner's uniquely turbulent and colorful career. There's a lovely irony in the bit about the changed identity: during these fateful years, as the composer entered the second half of his life, he was undergoing one of his profoundest transformations, teeming with new projects and preparing himself for what would become a more lasting revolution in art. Later, Wagner tried to downplay the extent of his actual involvement in the Dresden uprising when the patronage of the art-obsessed King Ludwig of Bavaria gave him a newfound appreciation of monarchy. Setting the revisionist pattern for generations of fans and foes to come—and more persuasively than any of them—Wagner was eager to refashion his image according to what he found most expedient at the time.

The topic of his involvement in the Revolution epitomizes a quality attaching to just about everything associated with Wagner. Whether the issue is his biography, his personality and beliefs, his rambling acres of prose, or (what really matters) his artistic legacy, we find everywhere a trait of overdetermination: overdetermination in the sense that Wagner constantly invites an abundance of interpretations and revisions, often mutually contradictory. And no matter how profuse these attempts to understand Wagner are, they fail to exhaust not just the significance of what he represents but our desire to get to the bottom of it. Even in an era that has made controversy blasé, Wagner continues to court it—and retains the ever rarer capacity to shock and overwhelm. How could we expect less from an artist who, without intending hyperbole, set out to fuse the achievements of Shakespeare and Beethoven into an "artwork of the future"?

With Wagner, the amount of factual and circumstantial knowledge isn't always proportional to our deeper understanding. There are mountains of such data. We know more about him than we do about almost anyone else in the pantheon of artists. As a human being, Wagner's degree of self-absorption makes the stereotypical Angeleno seem like a Trappist monk. Had he had access to the Internet, Wagner would dominate the blogosphere. On top of his colossal music dramas and the voluminous prose works that are their dubious shadow, Wagner somehow managed to compose a lengthy autobiography and some 10,000 letters. Add to this further tomes of witness from the obsessive diaries of his second wife Cosima and the recollections of his extensive circle of followers. Imagine if we had a similar amount of primary source material from Bach, Shakespeare, Da Vinci, or Mozart, cataloguing their every opinion—to what degree would this kind of intimate information shift our profile of these iconic artists?

In the case of Wagner, we might well ask exactly the opposite: if we knew less about the man, would the controversy surrounding his art be at all diminished? One certain result would be to erase the urgent need to separate the creator from his creations. The vast repertoire of facts notwithstanding, few artists remain so enmeshed in a network of legends, half-truths, hearsay, and misunderstanding. This was certainly the situation among Wagner's contemporaries; in large part, it still holds true today. How strange that much of the controversy relates to Wagner the man, the stunningly failed human being—even in our deconstructive era, which proclaims the "death of the author" and derides the biographical reading of a work of art as hopelessly old-fashioned.

But because of his insatiable narcissism and because of the disturbing, outrageously offensive reputation Wagner's personality has broadcast—noted, in self-congratulatory hindsight, with perhaps a slight touch of schadenfreude—we simply cannot resist the urge to investigate the convoluted circuitry tying together the man and the music. Often, when it comes to Wagner's famously disagreeable personality, a sort of circular logic ensues. We marvel at the astonishing thoroughness of his egotism. A paradigm of megalomania, Wagner's self-centeredness is so routinely pointed out that it tends to overshadow the far more fascinating paradox: that such obsessive individualism could produce an art with universal resonance. The egotism is indeed pervasive. It results in the endless theo-rizing that naturally posits Wagner's own art as the necessary culmination of a long evolutionary process. And it extends to the breathless chutzpah of his behavior, including the love affairs with his benefactors' wives—still as hardy a topic for gossip as it was in the cartoons of contemporary journals. Yet as we express shock, we pretend to ignore that without his exaggerated egotism, it's highly unlikely Wagner would have possessed the sheer will and resilience to realize his equally exaggerated artistic ambitions.

That's the more obvious silver lining of Wagnerian self-absorption. On a deeper level yet, what it seems to have enabled is an extraordinarily rare capacity for emotional intensity and engagement. And this is one of the central keys to understand-ing Wagner—both as man *and* as artist. His self-absorption wasn't a simple kind of one-note vanity but embraced a wide, tempestuous spectrum of states, not least of which were debili-tating bouts of suicidal despair. Wagner's way of perceiving other people and the world around him was always filtered through an almost unimaginable level of hypersensitivity. Even his range of intellectual preoccupations—a decisive and unique factor in his makeup as an artist—always emerged as a form of "feeling." And feeling, for Wagner, was a holistic faculty to which "thinking" was subordinate.

The immediacy that results is one of the reasons that people with no particular background in classical music can listen to Wagner—at least in smaller doses—and soon find themselves at ease with his musical language. Certainly his contemporaries were well aware of this phenomenon. The emotional wallop of Wagner's music was first encountered, it should not be forgot-ten, long before the convenience of recorded technology, in live settings. Trips to the theater (the *Festspielhaus*) he established in the sleepy town of Bayreuth in Bavaria to perform his works were experienced as life-changing pilgrimages. A nineteen-year-old Mahler wrote breathlessly of emerging from the *Festspielhaus* with the sense that "the greatest and most painful revelation had just been made to me, and that I would carry it unspoiled all my life."

To his contemporaries Wagner became a focal point for a kind of culture war in the second half of the nineteenth century. The debate inspired cults of disciples and opponents, each rallying around or denouncing the aesthetic world view that became known as Wagnerism. One of his most significant and persistent critics, Eduard Hanslick (whose observations are often brilliantly penetrating), observed that "Wagner's music affects the soul less than the nerves; it is not moving so much as eternally exciting, painfully concentrated, sensually and poetically exquisite." Hanslick was writing about *Lohengrin,* the last opera Wagner completed before his involvement in the Dresden Revolution. It became the most performed work in his lifetime. Referring to his early work on the *Ring,* Wagner himself said, "I imagine my music must be terrible; it is a morass of horrors and sublimities."

At its height, this cultural debate pitted Brahms against Wagner as the two figureheads for polar approaches to music. The former was advanced at masterfully preserving the best of tradition and engaging in "absolute music," carrying no pretensions beyond its own beauty and inner coherence but demanding a rigorous grounding in the language of music. Opponents of Wagner portrayed him as opening the floodgates to amateurs by practicing a kind of musical sorcery that titillated the senses. His demand for an art with visionary sway meant to redeem society appeared to them absurdly to arrogate dimensions having nothing to do with music. That aspect of the debate has long been outdated and seems silly now, even quaint.

But what still resonates is the image of Wagner as a dangerous musical pusher who concocted art saturated with an irresistibly narcotic power.

No one expressed this better than the philosopher Friedrich Nietzsche. An ardent disciple whose early work was deeply imprinted with the master's spirit, Nietzsche grew disillusioned and became Wagner's most bitter critic: "Is Wagner a human being at all? Is he not rather a disease? He contaminates everything he touches—he has made music sick." Nietzsche's complaints prefigure some of the attacks that would be aimed nearly a century later at the emerging phenomenon of rock music, which similarly threatened to sweep away all that had come before it. The equation of rock stars with the dangers of narcotic allurements have long since become cliché. (An offshoot of the image of Wagnerian music as a drug persists in the widespread perception that it is somehow too "heavy"—dietary metaphors here simply replace those of drugs and neurasthenic pills.) In an odd way, this objection to Wagner actually reinforces one of the composer's own central obsessions: that his music is not for casual consumption as a commodity of entertainment but is meant to transform and heighten consciousness.

In the wake of the First World War, the debate over what Wagner meant shifted focus into distinctly nonmusical areas. By then the music itself had long been assimilated into the progressive line of the narrative of Western art. Even the most professedly anti-Wagnerian of the early modernist composers—above all, Debussy and Stravinsky—betray the subtle influence this musical magician could still exert. Debussy does so by subliminally internalizing the more ambiguous aspects of Wagnerian tonality, while Stravinsky's bold, parodistic reversals and denial of all Wagner stood for are imbued with the energy of protest against an icon.

Now it was the significant theme of German nationalism in Wagner's proclamations—and by extension, in his musical works—that became a subject of suspicion. And yet, in a manner we will come to see is fundamentally Wagnerian, the correspondence between the works and new interpretations inspired by the changing times often has a surprisingly encompassing flexibility. For despite Wagner's heated pride in the destiny of German culture (a huge topic in itself, full of inconsistency and not always uncritical), could it not be seen that in his *Ring* cycle—that presumed glorification of Teutonic identity—Wagner actually foresees the destruction of civilization that was the experience of a century of two world wars?

But the Wagner debate that preoccupies us today was now entering its most disturbing chapter. Exhibit A in any discussion of the man-versus-art dilemma remains the composer's virulent anti-Semitism. After a century of self-indulgent artists in the public eye, from Picasso (whose womanizing truly dwarves the legendary exploits usually associated with Wagner) to Mick Jagger, we've grown accustomed to separating objectionable personal behavior from the art produced. If anything, we tend to assume one needs the other. Once Hitler declared Wagner his favorite composer, however, the stakes became altogether different. It's true that Wagner shared the fate of Beethoven, Nietzsche, and other cultural icons of being co-opted and twisted by the Nazis as a veneer for legitimacy. But as the Nazi catastrophe unfolded, the abhorrent racism that does thread through the composer's writings (and now tends to overshadow the genuinely progressive core ideas they also express) could no longer be swept away as mere eccentricity or the embarrassing vestige of a less enlightened age.

Not that such attempts have been lacking. At their most naïve, they imagine Wagner's works as colorful fairy tales set to unusually vivid music. But inevitably this has been answered by a swing in the opposite direction. There is now a cottage industry of studies purporting to reveal anti-Semitism as the very core and raison d'être for all of Wagner's art. The philosopher Theodor Adorno, having personally witnessed the evil of the Third Reich, was among the first critically to investigate this repellent aspect of Wagner in his stimulating *Versuch über Wagner* (In Search of Wagner). Since Robert Gutman's influential biography appeared in the 1960s, interpretations of Wagner's work as infected with the insidious ideas of racism (particularly of his last years) have been in the ascendancy. Studies by Hartmut Zelinsky and Marc Weiner in particular construct powerfully detailed readings to argue for the "anti-Semitic imagination" as a shaping force in Wagner's artistic configuration of a number of his villains—although it's important to realize that his villains are rarely conventional black-and-white ones.

Certainly it's a cop-out to whisk the issue away as a "suburban prejudice"—to use the apologetic phrase Ezra Pound applied to himself in an interview with Allen Ginsberg. In fact, Wagner's anti-Semitism can hardly be explained as an unfortunate by-product of his time. The composer himself, in the wake of his infamous essay "Das Judentum in der Musik" (Judaism in Music), confessed in one letter to a ruffled Franz Liszt that "this resentment is as necessary to my nature as gall is to the blood."

And yet the truth remains elusive. No one has convincingly managed to explain the strange intensity of Wagner's theoretical anti-Semitism (not to mention his vehement hatred of the French and of Jesuits) and the fact that it managed to coexist with admiration for the crucial role played by Jewish interpreters of his work (such as Hermann Levi, conductor of *Parsifal*'s premiere). Thought experiment: if we had no knowledge of Wagner's anti-Semitic beliefs, would it occur to us that they exist in the operas? As with all such single-focus examinations and reductions—and Wagner, for various reasons, seems to invite these more than almost any other artist—the larger context is easily lost.

Disingenuous denial of the appalling elements in Wagner's makeup is hardly necessary. But his art is not propaganda. It's hard to think of a musical dramatist who relies more thoroughly on ambiguity (on both the musical and dramatic levels). In fact, the Nazis discovered for themselves just how useless Wagner-as-propaganda-tool for their fellow thugs was, let alone for "the people." Mandatory performances bored the daylights out of soldiers on leave, while the *Ring* cycle, with its deconstruction of the desire for world domination and enslavement, could hardly be expected to inspire as the war turned against them. Stagings of the pacifist-oriented *Parsifal* were meanwhile banned for the duration. What matters ultimately, of course, is the experience of Wagner's works as art: if these were mere envelopes for propaganda, encoding hideous doctrines, how could they possibly continue to resonate?

Audiences have been wrestling with Wagner's musical expression, his characters, and their underlying significance since they first took to the stage. Of Wagner the hapless, deeply flawed man, a plethora of images coexist and blend uncomfortably: the socialist revolutionary and reformer; the pan-German nationalist; the sensitive human being who preached an evangelical vegetarianism anticipating the animal rights and environmental movements; the proto-Nazi favored by Hitler, whose music (specifically, *Tannhäuser*) was claimed by Zionism's founder, Theodore Herzl, to have inspired him with his epiphany of the Jewish State; the vainglorious megalomaniac who yet wrote at length of his desire to commit suicide; the politically engaged artist who became the idol of the art-for-art's-sake movement; the arch-Romantic obsessed with an idealized version of impossible love who could portray the cynical mechanisms of *Realpolitik* with a flair that would have brought a smile to Machiavelli. The list goes on. For Debussy, in a telling phrase, he was "a beautiful sunset that was mistaken for a dawn." And yet his influence was so profound that it extended well beyond music to leading figures in other disciplines. To give just a brief sampling: Baudelaire and the later Symbolists; Thomas Mann, Marcel Proust, and George Bernard Shaw; innumerable theater and film directors; even—by way of what Mann would call a "panegyric in reverse"—his vociferous detractor Bertolt Brecht.

Still, however heated the controversy has been, there is a sense in which we've all become Wagnerians now. Think of the success of composers such as John Williams, or James Horner and Howard Shore, with their tightly integrated themes and prismatically arrayed orchestrations for films of epic, Wagnerian ambition. Think too of how resonant those very films have been in the larger culture, responding to a shared need for myth and psychology to rely on in our "disenchanted" postmodern world.

Wagner is, after all, our mirror, the ultimate Janus face. The more closely we live with his works and get to know them over time, the more intensely they reflect back aspects of ourselves—aspects that may have been hidden but can gain clarity as we confront the crises of our own lives reflected in the music dramas. The following attempts to shed a modest light on this mysterious process. If it sparks any desire for further exploration, it will have succeeded.

Setting the Stage
Wagner's Emergence as an Artist

The key to approaching Wagner is to realize that, above everything else, he is a man of the theater. His artistic vision is inseparable from the theatrical world of heightened reality. The revolutionary pursuit of the artwork of the future and musical reform, the philosophical ideas he internalized, the ongoing quest for redemption explored in his works—all these inevitably are filtered through the prism of theater's magic. For Wagner, theater provides the vessel to transcend a compromised world and to commune most profoundly with an audience in a quasi-sacramental directness.

Describing his childhood enthusiasms in *Mein Leben* (My Life), the autobiography composed in 1864 for his new mistress Cosima and his new patron King Ludwig, Wagner attributes the early allure of theater (understood to include the world of music theater and opera) to "a tingling delight in finding myself in an atmosphere that represented such a contrast to normal life by its purely fantastic and almost appallingly attractive quality." His theater-mania might be seen from another angle as well: in the propensity for shape-shifting that Wagner exhibited throughout his life, masterfully playing the part required by drastic changes in circumstance.

He grew up, after all, in a household dominated by theater. Born Wilhelm Richard Wagner on May 22, 1813, he was officially the ninth (and last) child of a bureaucrat of the Leipzig police force, Friedrich Wagner. These were extraordinary and dangerous times. Outside the city, massive armies were poised for some of the decisive confrontations of the Napoleonic era, which raged over the ensuing months. Against this backdrop of scenes Tolstoy would later paint so vividly in *War and Peace,* Richard's mother, Johanna, had meanwhile crossed through enemy lines with her new baby. She found refuge to the east in Bohemia with a close family friend, Ludwig Geyer. Napoleon was finally routed that fall in the Battle of the Nations. A month later, Friedrich Wagner became a victim of the disease spreading from the carnage that resulted. He contracted typhus and died prematurely, just six months after Richard's birth. Geyer, playing a sort of guardian angel to the destitute Johanna, helped at first to keep the family together; the following year, the two were married.

Arising from these dramatic circumstances, a phenomenal amount of speculation has been invested in the issue of which man was Wagner's biological father (even further complication stems from more recent evidence that Johanna had had an affair with a local prince). The consensus seems to be that neither case can be conclusively proved. Wagner himself has left plenty of evidence indicating he thought it possible that Geyer was his father. Much of the fascination here revolves around the belief, once prevalent but apparently unfounded, that Geyer was of Jewish origin. (Ironically, given his wildly anti-Semitic beliefs, Wagner's birthplace was in the Brühle, the Jewish Quarter of Leipzig.) In any event, the biological reality is superseded by the psychological: the question mark around his paternity will have a profound resonance in Wagner's operas. It takes the form of an identity crisis that his heroes face over and over, typically centered around an absent or abandoning father. But it should be noted too that—despite Wagner's affectionate descriptions of his mother, who died in 1848—longing for an absent mother (expressed by Siegfried and Parsifal) inspires some of his most poignant musical effusions.

Ludwig Geyer certainly played the role of father to young Richard. His early death from tuberculosis in 1821 was a terrible loss. Wagner's later descriptions of this "most noble benefactor" are suffused with genuine warmth. Friedrich Wagner, an inveterate theater buff, had introduced Geyer into the family as a close friend. Geyer was a talented man of the theater who had success essentially as a character actor (he was especially well known for his villains). But, as if anticipating his stepson's multiple artistic personalities, he was also a poet and playwright. One of his plays was reportedly admired by Goethe. Geyer was moreover sufficiently respected as a painter to earn significant income from portrait commissions. His painting helped him get through his early years as a wandering, homeless actor trying to make it (his days of hardship also anticipate Wagner's years of wandering). As stepfather, Geyer left a deep imprint on the household, thanks to his artistic temperament. He relocated the family to the artistically vibrant city of Dresden, where he was a member of the resident theater company as "court actor." Several of Wagner's siblings ended up pursuing a life in the theater as opera singers. (As mentioned above, during this period, "theater" meant the institution that presented both spoken drama and opera.) Amusingly, Geyer envisioned a future for young Richard as a painter (one of the few arts for which Wagner made no claim to having talent). While Geyer was on his deathbed, the eight-year-old timidly played a bit at the piano to ease his suffering. Wagner remarks that Geyer then asked his mother, "Could it be that he has a talent for music?"

That talent, however, remained in the background for a while. Wagner is among the least musically precocious of the great composers. His journey toward music was via a roundabout path—through the world of theater and literature. A favorite pastime was creating performances for the puppet theater Geyer left for the children. Wagner also recalls spending time at his stepfather's workplace as a youngster, backstage and in the "concealed loge," from which he observed Geyer playing a number of villains. Little Richard even began to participate in the proceedings onstage. One anecdote in *Mein Leben* concerns his debut in a play with incidental music by Carl Maria von Weber (Kapellmeister of the Dresden Opera, a post that Wagner himself would take over in 1843): "I recall figuring in a tableau vivant as an angel, entirely sewn up in tights and with wings on my back, in a graceful, though laboriously learned, pose."

Wagner meanwhile began to develop a serious love of literature under the influence of his reclusive but progressively inclined uncle, the scholar-translator-poet Adolf Wagner. Richard was a fitful student, ignoring what bored him and often getting in trouble for extended periods of truancy. But he excelled when he was able to throw himself enthusiastically into his latest passion. One such passion was the world of classical Greece and mythology. As a schoolboy, Wagner translated half of *The Odyssey*. He also began on an epic poem about the Muses and sketched a play based on the death of Ulysses. Shakespeare was another mania, together with Goethe's *Faust* and the weird fantasy world of E. T. A. Hoffmann (this Romantic visionary, it should be recalled, explored his aspirations as both a writer and an opera composer in a kind of assimilation that Wagner would later enact).

Wagner drew on all these passions and amalgamated them into a major endeavor at age fifteen: a "vast tragic drama" titled *Leubald und Adelaide.* He wrote his manuscript in a distinctively stylized calligraphy of backward-bent letters, which one of his teachers compared to "Persian cuneiform." Uncle Adolf apparently failed to disguise his horror at this product of the Gothic teen's imagination and feared literature would prove a baneful influence. Wagner, as he recalled it later in *Mein Leben,* had more or less combined elements of *Hamlet, King Lear, Macbeth,* and Goethe's *Götz von Berlichingen* wholesale. By the last act, so many corpses had accumulated on stage that, to conclude the drama, they had to return as ghosts.

But this exercise provided a remarkable epiphany for Wagner: "I knew what no one else could understand, namely that my work could only be judged rightly when provided with the *music* I had now decided to write for it and which I intended to start composing immediately." From this revelation, Wagner dates his desire to learn the art of music. And what this meant at the very beginning was to compose; he wasn't interested in any kind of performing career and never mastered an instrument (his piano style was highly idiosyncratic): music was perceived as a means to an end. Wagner repeatedly emphasized the autodidactic aspect of his knowledge. Clearly he spent endless hours poring over scores of Beethoven, the Mozart of the Requiem, and contemporaries such as Weber. He wanted above all to be understood as a "natural" talent that hadn't been constrained by the bonsailike training of routine musical exercise. Indeed he did begin a self-guided study, borrowing a book on counterpoint whose overdue fines must count as the first in a long line of debts he allowed to spin out of control. But the claim that he was all but self-taught is a typical example of Wagnerian exaggeration. In fact his musical education did entail more systematic grounding in the rules of counterpoint and harmonic theory than he later acknowledged.

Another watershed was his discovery of Beethoven—particularly of the Ninth Symphony, which he learned inside-out by making a piano transcription in 1830 (just six years after the work had been premiered in Vienna). A similarly seminal breakthrough was his encounter with the art of soprano Wilhelmine Schröder-Devrient. Her commitment to both the vocal and dramatic aspects of her roles enhanced her reputation as the Maria Callas of her time. Wagner took to her performances as pure revelation. Immediately after he first saw her on stage (his claim that she had played the heroine Leonore in Beethoven's *Fidelio* possibly involves some typical anecdotal spinning on Wagner's part), he wrote a breathless letter of thanks to the stunned soprano, declaring she had made clear his future path.

Curiously, given the original impetus that led the teenage Wagner to undertake composition, he first gravitated toward instrumental forms, writing a series of sonatas, a string quartet, various overtures, and a rather successful symphony. He began, in other words, precisely with the sort of abstract, absolute music that he later declared was dead. As far as we know, the first public performance of Wagner (although it was given anonymously) occurred on Christmas Eve in 1830. It must have been an unforgettable moment of humiliation, and Wagner's account in *Mein Leben* is priceless.

The piece, which was simply called "New Overture," was an essay in B-flat directly influenced by Beethoven's Ninth. The young composer had given "mystical significance" to his orchestra, which he divided into opposing forces of brass, strings, and winds (these were to be symbolized by different inks in the score: black, red, and green respectively, although he was unable to locate any green ink). Apparently the main "red" theme in the violins took up four bars; but after every occurrence of the theme an incongruous thump from the timpani was then scored in the following bar. No matter how intriguing the mixture of themes from the "red," "green," or "black" instruments, the timpani continued its fifth-bar intrusion relentlessly. Wagner became aware to his horror that the audience found this thump all too predictable: "I heard my neighbors calculating and announcing the returning beat in advance: my sufferings, knowing the correctness of these calculations, defy description. I lost consciousness." It was to be Wagner's first, but far from last, musical fiasco. The chagrined composer returned home to open Christmas presents at "the brilliant family festivities, which lit with grim irony the black night of my stupefaction."

In 1832 Wagner contemplated his first opera, which significantly integrated his coexisting desires as writer and composer. Given his development thus far, there was nothing extraordinary about Wagner playing dual roles as librettist and composer—which would, of course, set the pattern he followed in all his subsequent works. Inspired by a medieval legend, he first sketched out the idea for an E. T. A. Hoffmannesque novella (in which music would play a crucial thematic role). The story involved a fateful wedding day. A mysterious guest appears, and his relation to the bride is the catalyst for the tragedy. Meanwhile, an old organist keeps watch over all the characters' secrets but in the end is found dead on his organ bench: "after playing an impressive requiem and expiring during an endlessly prolonged triad at its close." Wagner didn't finish his novella but decided to use the nocturnal and grim story for an opera to be called *Die Hochzeit* (The Wedding). He got as far as a few numbers before his sister Rosalie showed distaste for the libretto, at which point he abandoned the project.

Meanwhile, Wagner had taken his first professional musical job as chorus master at the theater in Würzburg (a post facilitated by family connections, since his elder brother Albert was now a tenor). He saw his next project through to completion: *Die Feen* (The Fairies), his official first opera. For his source, Wagner turned to a fable, *La donna serpente* (The Serpent Woman), by the classical Venetian playwright Carlo Gozzi. Gozzi has more famously entered the operatic repertoire as the author of the stories behind *Turandot* (originally a commedia dell'arte fable) and the Strauss-Hofmannstahl masterpiece *Die Frau ohne Schatten* (The Woman without a Shadow). Wagner may have been prescient in that respect; but his first opera, frankly, doesn't go very far in predicting the genius who was to emerge.

Some artists plant their flag remarkably early. Consider the very first symphonies of Beethoven, Mahler, and Shostakovich, for example. Each lays claim with his initial forays in the genre to a startling new voice: gateways opening up brave new worlds to come with utmost self-assurance. But even with precocious composers, a period of trial and error seems to be the more usual archetype for those tackling opera; so it was with Verdi and Puccini, who early suffered humiliating failures on the stage. All the more so for a late bloomer like Wagner. To be sure, Wagner's assimilation of musical knowledge was extraordinarily rapid. But years of maturing were yet to elapse before he would find his authentic musical voice in *Der fliegende Holländer* (The Flying Dutchman). Unlike the gradual accrual of confidence and security normally associated with the late bloomer—the path Brahms followed in his conquest of the symphonic form—Wagner's early development traces what evolutionary biologists might term a pattern of "punctuated equilibrium."

In *Die Feen*, Wagner lays claim to the period of German-Romantic opera that he had known since his first discoveries of Carl Maria von Weber—above all, *Der Freischütz* (The Sharpshooter). This is the post-Beethovenian style that marks some of the first attempts by German opera composers to forge a national opera in the face of the dominant genres of Italian *bel canto* (literally, "beautiful singing") and French grand opera. Like Weber—and Auber, Mendelssohn, and Marschner, other contemporary German composers who left their mark on the style—Wagner turned to the fantasy world of supernatural creatures. Gozzi's theatrical fable is a sort of retelling of the Orpheus myth, itself the core myth from which the very genre of opera originates. Prince Arindal falls in love with Ada, a fairy who is half mortal. A la Mozart's *The Magic Flute,* Arindal is subjected to a number of trials in order to remain united with his beloved—and fails miserably. He is forbidden to ask who she is but does so and later is driven to curse her. Ada ultimately must pay the price by being turned to stone (rather than the snake of Gozzi's original). Arindal's loss drives him to insanity, yet when he pursues Ada into the underworld, his song revives her. The pair are allowed to unite as Arindal renounces his kingdom among mortals and joins Ada among the fairies.

In the sense of mimicking a recognized style, Wagner at age twenty shows an impressive aptitude: the score deftly weaves together the conventional interplay between recitative numbers (in which dialogue is composed in a manner more closely approximating speech rhythms) and set numbers (including extensive and lively writing for complex ensembles, such as a septet and chorus). There's emotional vividness in several of the solo numbers, although nothing really distinctly memorable. Interestingly, Wagner does invest the recitative with an unusual amount of energy via punctuating percussion, as if to foreshadow his desire to elevate the recitative to a higher dramatic level.

If there is little noticeably Wagnerian about the music of *Die Feen,* its story gives us perhaps a closer sense of his true voice. The contact between human and immortal realms that precipitates a crisis sounds a characteristic Wagnerian note: we will encounter this repeatedly, most obviously in *Tannhäuser, Lohengrin* (which shares the motive of the forbidden question), and the *Ring* cycle. Moreover, the crisis leads to a search for redemption from it, which is achieved only through the power of love: the resounding theme of all of Wagner's works to come. It's intriguing to note how closely Wagner already approaches his dramatic preoccupations before discovering the musical means to give them fullest expression.

Although he managed to complete his first opera, Wagner was fated to see it languish unproduced (it received a posthumous premiere in 1888). Yet the act of writing *Die Feen* already exorcised a need to prove he could create German opera in the accepted contemporary style. Wagner apparently then experienced an aesthetic change of heart—no doubt abetted by his increasing exposure to the beauties of bel canto opera by Bellini, whose music he would continue to treasure. He describes his shift in allegiance from "abstract mysticism" represented by the Weberian, Gothic world of German opera to the "material" and "witty" world of Mediterranean opera. His early essay "Die deutsche Oper" (On German Opera) castigated his countrymen for sticking to artificial, pedantic notions of opera, while Wagner expressed his praise for Bellini in an essay of that name in 1837.

Abiding as his adolescent love of Shakespeare had been, what Wagner chose as source for his next opera project was not one of the Bard's great tragedies, then in particular vogue, but the "problem comedy" *Measure for Measure.* Shakespeare's complex exploration of the nature of hypocrisy and the division between true justice and the law would in any case offer an extraordinary challenge to adapt to the reigning conventions of the opera stage. Wagner's approach was to focus on the strictures against natural sensuality imposed by the hypocritical Puritanism of the ruler Friedrich. He renames the story *Das Liebesverbot* (The Ban on Love) and relocates Shakespeare's original setting of Vienna to Palermo—the Mediterranean locale presumably being more suitable for the opera's sun-kissed message of sexual liberation and a society devoted to pleasure.

Das Liebesverbot stands out as a rare comedy in Wagner's list of works. He would return to this genre only in his original concept for the opera known as *Siegfried* and in his mature masterpiece *Die Meistersinger*. *Die Feen* had been a "grand romantic opera," while his second endeavor was a two-act "grand comic opera." Wagner's aesthetic change of heart is evident in the Italianate aspects of his melodic imagination here, particularly in fleshing out the soprano role of Isabella, sister of the nobleman Claudio, who has been condemned to die merely for loving. Wagner had introduced some recurring motives in *Die Feen* (a technique clearly used by Weber and other early Romantics to evoke a certain atmosphere, such as the demonic Samiel in *Der Freischütz*). *Das Liebesverbot* carries this technique a little further, most clearly with its readily identifiable motive for the curse on love that is lifted by Isabella's strategy.

Thematically, Wagner's adaptation of Shakespeare shows more keenly his idiosyncratic take on source material. This will become a recurrent pattern. It is characteristic of his approach to the mythic sources that inform so much of his future work. Thus Isabella figures as an early prototype for the redeeming woman (who incidentally also portrays the good common sense associated with *Die Meistersinger*'s Eva). The opera's denouement, which results in a Woodstock-like era of free love as the hypocritical Friedrich is unmasked, also points to the overcoming of a corrupt reign that inspired Wagner's early conception of the *Ring*.

Wagner began composing the music for *Das Liebesverbot* in early 1835, taking about a year to complete it. During this time, he had become music director of a motley troupe of itinerant thespians and singers run by a bankrupt impresario. Among its prima donnas was an attractive heartbreaker of a soprano named Christine Wilhelmine Planer. *Mein Leben* claims that Wagner in fact joined the company to pursue her. Four years younger, he had been enjoying the life of a young Bohemian rake, but he became increasingly obsessed with "Minna," as she was known. Their stormy courtship presaged a far storm- ier marriage. Wagner wooed Minna while the misfortunate Bethmann company staged the premiere of his new opera. At least this time Wagner was able to bring his work before the public (in March 1836), but the evening was a fiasco to compare with the "New Overture" premiere. Some of the cast apparently failed to learn their roles, while a lovers' quarrel led to a fist fight with the lead tenor backstage. Opening night was closing as well for *Das Liebesverbot*.

Wagner did however manage to win Minna—for the time being, that is—and the two wed later that fall. Eventually the Bethmann company went belly up, Minna split for a new lover, and Wagner landed a job in 1837 as musical director for the theater in Riga (in present-day Latvia, then a Russian out- post heavily colonized by Germans). He prevailed on Minna to rejoin him, swearing to her that his big break was about to come. In fact Wagner contemplated yet another comedy (plan- ning a Mozart-like *Singspiel* based on a story from *The Arabian Nights*) but dropped that for what seemed a surefire path to success: a tragic work modeled on French grand opera. This was Wagner's third complete opera, *Rienzi, der letzte der Tribunen* (Rienzi, the Last of the Tribunes), which is the first of his works to have gotten a toehold in the repertory. It's actually possible to encounter performances of *Rienzi* today, while the first two operas are complete rarities on stage.

The source in this case wasn't a preexisting play but a then- popular novel by the British Edward Bulwer-Lytton. Like *Die Feen* and *Das Liebesverbot*, Wagner studiously modeled *Rienzi* after available prototypes in the opera world of his time. This time, less as an aesthetic shift of taste, he had chosen French grand opera as his likeliest route to make a mark. Wagner desperately wanted to escape Riga (he soon had to in order to flee his creditors) and try his luck in Paris, the opera capital of the world at the time. *Rienzi* was to be his ticket to fame. Wagner read the novel in 1837 and began working out his operatic version the following year. He brought the score-in-progress along as he and Minna made their precarious journey from Riga to Paris. There Wagner would spend what he recalled as the most miserable years of his life (between 1839 and 1842).

Rienzi was constructed from a historical novel set in fourteenth-century Rome. Its involved plot centers on a fundamental conflict between groups of rival patricians and the populist Cola Rienzi, who promises to restore the forgotten virtues of the classical Roman Republic, with much of the action arising from the quest for vengeance. The easily duped populace is led to turn against Rienzi (a move engineered by the Church) and their agitation results in his downfall. In the manner of French grand opera, Wagner ensures a steady succession of impressive numbers, following the gamut from soul-baring arias to conflicted trios and powerfully paced full ensembles.

Musically, *Rienzi* comes off as remarkably self-confident, a work that sounds very much like opera of the period but not yet quite like Wagner. Its best-known melody (spotlit in the overture and the basis for the hero's act 5 aria "Allmächtiger Vater" [Almighty Father]) hints of the motive that will be associated with Brünnhilde-as-woman in the *Ring* cycle's final opera, while a recurrent trumpet call and the motive associated with the desire for revenge bring us even closer to the *leitmotif* (literally, "leading or guiding motive") system we will later encounter. And the opera's climactic scene, which involves the visually extravagant effect of the Capitol being set ablaze and its tower collapsing, has its obvious echo in the final scene of *Götterdämmerung*.

Yet for all that, *Rienzi* still feels like Wagner adapting himself to preexisting formulas rather than adapting them to his unique voice. *Mein Leben* suggests how calculated were his efforts to "outdo all previous examples with sumptuous extravagance." His begrudging admiration for the masters of the style, Meyerbeer and Halevy, is evident particularly in the earlier parts of the opera. Despite the nasty insults he later sallied against Meyerbeer as his bête noir of everything wrong with opera, Wagner would in fact continue his borrowings from the genre of grand opera even in his most Wagnerian creations. Indeed, he continued work on the opera as he was trying to use Meyerbeer's connections to gain entrée to the Paris Opera, finishing the score in 1840.

Wagner didn't manage to get *Rienzi* (or his other operas) performed at the opera world's nerve center. But he did finally achieve the breakthrough he was hoping for when—thanks in part to Meyerbeer's lobbying on his behalf—the Dresden Opera decided to give the premiere in 1842. After the fiasco of *Das Liebesverbot,* he had deliberately planned *Rienzi* on an extravagant scale so it couldn't be attempted by small-fry provincial ensembles. Indeed, the premiere of this five-act "grand tragic opera" in October 1842 reportedly lasted over six hours. Yet it was Wagner's first hit (and remained one into the late nineteenth century, to his embarrassment). The tremendous success of that premiere paved the way for Wagner to land a new position as assistant music director at the Dresden Court Opera, which he held from 1843 until the Revolution in 1849.

The return trip from Paris back to Germany filled Wagner with elation (and gave him one of his first concrete impressions for the opera that would become *Tannhäuser*). But the tempest-tossed trip that took him to Paris in the first place—according, at least, to the composer's account in *Mein Leben*—also provided the seed for the work that would prove to be his true artistic breakthrough, as will soon be seen.

Navigating a Way into Wagner

Der fliegende Holländer

The first forays Wagner made into opera contain hints of his real voice. But they're well disguised behind the mask of conventional styles and formulas the composer was assimilating—or rather, trying on. The reverse happens with *Der fliegende Holländer* (The Flying Dutchman), the first opera that feels and *sounds* authentically Wagnerian. Here the composer's unique musical and dramatic vision begins to coalesce so strikingly that its reliance on convention often recedes into the background. For the opera signals an extraordinarily confident leap: a new way of bringing drama to life through music in an amalgam that expresses Wagner's deepest preoccupations. It's a leap surpassed only when the composer embarks on the *Ring* with his music for *Das Rheingold*.

Even before completing *Rienzi,* Wagner had been attracted to the legend of the Flying Dutchman as an ideal topic for an opera. He later recounted how it had personally affected him during a rough and perilous voyage through the North Sea in 1839, as he was making his way from Riga to Paris. It wasn't just the story, with its supernatural aura, that resonated. Wagner describes how an initial musical impulse came to him once the tiny storm-tossed ship in which he, his wife Minna, and his beloved Newfoundland dog Robber were sailing found safe haven among the Norwegian fjords.

The composer's constant narrative recasting of the genesis of his works, written in hindsight, should naturally be considered with skepticism—especially in the case of his earlier, more conventional operas. In his various letters, essays, and particularly his lengthy autobiography *Mein Leben*, Wagner was increasingly at pains to argue for an inevitable, "organic" line of development in his art, smoothing over awkward gaps and inconvenient facts. But even bearing such caution in mind, we have no need to doubt why this material attracted him: "A primal trait of human nature speaks out from [the figure of the Flying Dutchman].... This trait, in its most universal meaning, is the longing after rest from amid the storms of life."

Wagner refers to the plight of the Dutchman that lies at the basis of the folk legend. The Dutchman (tellingly, he remains unnamed in Wagner's version, perhaps as the embodiment of an archetype; he is called "Vanderdecken" elsewhere) is a sea captain accompanied by a similarly ghostly crew. He has been condemned to roam the world in his ship until Judgment Day for challenging Satan during a storm. Another crucial element ensured that the subject would fascinate Wagner. This was the spin given by the poet Heinrich Heine in a passage within a fictional memoir he published in 1833, *Aus den Memoiren des Herren von Schnabelewopski* (From the Memoirs of Herr von Schnabelewopski). Heine had introduced the idea of the Dutchman's bid for release from this cursed eternal cycle through the agency of a woman's love: if the Dutchman can find a woman willing to be faithful "unto death," he will be freed from his wandering. Heine's twist was meant as ironic and actually cast a cynical eye on the love extolled by Romanticism, already a literary cliché by this time. The woman in his story is mockingly called "Mrs. Flying Dutchman," with a moral appended as to the need to be vigilant about marrying seafaring strangers.

For Wagner, though, these two core elements, the curse
and the chance for redemption through love, had an urgent
and primary appeal. Heine's anti-Romantic defense mechanism
was irrelevant for him. The Dutchman's state of self-conscious
suffering, together with its possible resolution through a selfless love from a woman who rejects the conventions of her
surrounding society, suggested a potent fusion. It also fused
Wagner the dramatist and Wagner the composer into the kind
of unified aim that had been hitherto lacking. *Der fliegende
Holländer,* he said, marked the start of "my career as poet, and
my farewell to the mere concoctor of opera texts."

By "poet," Wagner seems to mean the creator of a dramatic
framework that isn't merely "set" to music but that is conceived
as part of a larger, integral whole completed by the music as a
richer dimension. In other words, this is the operatic work in
which Wagner recognizes that the relations between drama and
music, between words and singing, are embarking on a new
path (although it must be cautioned that they don't attain the
degree of integration he would have us believe in his later commentary). A symbolic reminder of this in-between quality—of
the opera as arising from inherited tradition but also looking
ahead to the uniquely Wagnerian—is its dual existence in inter-
missionless one-act and three-act versions. Wagner originally
intended a more concentrated experience via the former but
settled for the latter when the opera was actually premiered in
Dresden in January 1843.

Wagner after all labeled *Der fliegende Holländer* a "romantic
opera," an indication that he hadn't exactly stepped outside
the bounds of one of the prevailing contemporary genres.
The setting with its personified sea, and the apparition of the
Dutchman's ghost ship unfurling blood-red sails, along with
other references to the supernatural, contain stock elements
of the Gothic-horror side of the Romantic spirit. Yet Wagner

distances himself from standard-issue Romanticism in a number of telling ways. To begin, the narrative itself is sharply honed. It evidences a lean starkness, following the dramatic throughline with an intense focus. Even seemingly extraneous details, such as the Women's Spinning Chorus or the Norwegian sailors and their girls mocking the ghost ship's crew, are essential to establishing moods against which critical dramatic events emerge. Such economy no doubt springs in part from the modest intentions of the original plan for the opera (which was to be a curtain raiser to a ballet). Yet it points ahead to a crucial feature that Wagner will continue to perfect in subsequent works as they expand to fuller and more imposing dimensions. This is his desire to liberate the drama from the external trappings of conventional exposition so as to concentrate more fully on its aspect as *mythos* (an archetypal story that embodies universal truths).

Even more striking in its uniqueness is Wagner's portrayal of his title character. The composer may have begun by borrowing the undead figure of a popular tale, who made for a good ghost story. But he invested him with the mythic trappings of the legend of Ahasuerus, the Wandering Jew—one of the archetypal "outsider" figures who recur in Wagner's operas. On another level still, he echoes the straying, hapless soul of a familiar Romantic type, epitomized in the sublimely moving pathos of Lord Byron's Manfred. The latter (who was indeed a fertile source for composers such as Schumann and Tchaikovsky) endures a seemingly fathomless isolation and Faustian restlessness that make him cousin to the Dutchman. Wagner indeed gives his hero a monologue whose intensity wouldn't be out of place in *Manfred*. But in the realm of opera it strikes a pitch hitherto unheard. "Die Frist ist Um" (The time is up), his introductory monologue, lays out the Dutchman's plight, along with his one hope to escape from the repeated pattern of his curse through the selfless love of a woman.

Wagner's setting of this monologue is extraordinary—even given its broad outlines as an aria from the conventional *number opera* (this standard division of the text into solos, duets, trios, and choruses exists alongside *Der fliegende Holländer*'s innovative aspects). The premiere of the opera was by all accounts marred by an unsympathetic interpretation of the role by an incapable singer. But aside from that, the unusual effect of "Die Frist Ist Um" may have been something like what rock fans encountered when Dylan cast aside the formulaic lyrics of pop music and introduced a wholly new, serious kind of poetry. What might have been a piece of ordinary melodrama for a rote composer here becomes the takeoff point for a musical portrait of uncanny intensity. Wagner ratchets up the tension through ominously dark colorings and outbursts in the orchestra (this degree of intensity is already clearly present in the overture [CD 1, track 1]). The suffering endured by the Dutchman, in all its existential horror, is the true focus; its true cause remains significantly indeterminate. In his passionately argued book *Wagner,* the philosopher Michael Tanner identifies the Dutchman as the first in a lineage, the "prototype of the Wagnerian protagonist: someone who has done something so terrible that he has to spend the rest of his existence looking for salvation."

It doesn't take much of a leap to intuit a degree of self-portraiture in the Dutchman. As Wagner continues to mature, the self-portraits in his works become more complex, even at times split among several characters. Yet here the Dutchman figures not just as the archetype for an existential situation, nor even for the class of convention-defying explorers (by extension, artists), but on the most personal level for a young composer who had been buffeted by the slings and arrows of outrageous fashion. To this self-portrayal, however, Wagner adds a fascinatingly apt psychological insight. His Dutchman steers clear of a dangerously tempting self-pity. Wagner details the endless chain of suffering that is his lot, but he introduces the idea of hope, which will take the form of Senta, the opera's heroine. The Dutchman thus finds himself caught in a dilemma that Wagner continues to explore in his most complex heroes hereafter (especially Wotan and Amfortas): it is a pattern of cynical assumption that there is no way out, alleviated by a ray of hope. When that hope itself seems to die, the level of despair gains a far greater intensity.

The figure of Senta is Wagner's own invention and the first of a long line of original figures (particularly women) he interpolates into preexisting material from legend and myth. On the surface she might seem to be the epitome of schmaltzy Romanticism. Wagner's imperviousness to the brand of irony exemplified by his source Heine is often seen as a sort of Achilles heel for the composer. It's the sort of thing Nietzsche relished parodying (at one point he mocks the "Senta-mentality" of Wagner). This is a path full of fruitful possibility, from the chains of absurd narrative "logic" in the *Ring* cycle lampooned by Anna Russell to Charles Ludlam's delightful skewering in *Der Ring Gott Farblonjet* (a Yiddish parody meaning, roughly, "The Absolutely Confused Ring")—a campy, kitsch-packed, anarchic burlesque written for his Ridiculous Theatrical Company in the 1970s. The opera's finale, as the figures of Senta and the Dutchman become "transfigured" after their deaths and rise over the sea embracing each other, certainly has all the trappings of Romantic kitsch.

But that's if you take as literal what operates on a different plane entirely. Part of the confusion arises from the peculiar mixture of dramatic incident and musical content such as Wagner alone is able to create. Together, both reinforce a level of experience beyond realism, but one that can break down into incoherence when they are divorced. With regard to Senta, Wagner was actually aware of the problem and concerned to distance his heroine from the stereotypical, sentimental savior figure of Romanticism. In his notes on performing the opera, he says that Senta must not be played in such a way that "the dreamy side of her nature is conceived in the sense of a modern, sickly sentimentality." Indeed, "she is no longer the home-tending Penelope of Ulysses, as courted in the days of old, but the quintessence of womankind; and yet the still unmanifest, longed-for, dreamed-of, infinitely womanly woman...: the woman of the future." Senta is, in short, Wagner's operatic prototype for the all-important Romantic concept of "das ewig Weibliche" ("the eternal feminine" as Goethe termed it at the end of his *Faust*). He will refine this prototype as the key to the longed-for redemption explored in his works (although, contrary to what is often assumed, not the only way to achieve that redemption).

Wagner's pivotal duet between Senta and the Dutchman, when they finally meet (and nonnaturalistically declare their immediate love), is a central part of his strategy in making these characters matter to us, since both of them are outside our normal realm of experience (as they are indeed for the rest of the cast in the opera). The expansive feeling of this passage stretches beyond the confines of a single set number and shows Wagner thinking of larger units flowing together as one interconnected scene (some have called this a *scene opera,* as opposed to a number opera). Again, one shouldn't get carried away by seeing too much of the future Wagner already present, just as his use of a recurrent musical theme for the Dutchman is still rather mechanical and not part of an organic system. But the leisurely pacing of this duet does create a sense of stepping back from the mundane velocity of the world surrounding it, a kind of lyrical expanse of our perception of time that Wagner will perfect in *Tristan und Isolde*. It's almost as if the pair are expressing a shared hallucination—Wagner's take on the trope of lovers standing apart in their own world.

Some celebrated stagings have played up the hallucinatory quality that pervades the audience's firsthand experience of Senta's character. They present the entire opera as the result of the dream she describes in her ballad, a set number that tells the audience much about her. The Dutchman too appears in the context of the Steersman's drifting off to sleep, as if he were an emanation from the latter's active imagination. And the dream narrated by Senta's hapless boyfriend Erik hints even more of the eerie connections between what are apparently legends shared by this community and the actual internal life of Senta, who has absorbed them in a way that sets her apart. The effect at times anticipates the nonlinear, associative power of expressionist theater.

Senta is a twin to the Dutchman in her own alienation, not a passive sacrificial victim. She herself is shown to recognize this affinity, and her compassion for the Dutchman makes her suicide an act of her free will. It takes the Dutchman by surprise. He had resigned himself to disappointment but hoped to break at least one part of the pattern's cycle: by freeing Senta from her vow (the women who fail to remain true "unto death" become damned, suggesting a vampirelike quality to the Dutchman). Wagner accentuates this dramatic truth through an unmistakable musical dualism. In introducing both, he creates a unique, haunting sound world ("Die Frist Ist Um" and "Senta's Ballad") for these creatures apart, thus giving their set numbers an original twist. This is meant to contrast with the music surrounding them. The latter takes various forms to suggest a mundane, normal context to foreground their weirdness: the unselfconscious, businesslike melody of the bourgeois father Daland (ready to offer Senta in marriage when tempted by the Dutchman's boasted wealth), the sailors' joyful shanty-rhythms, the pleasantly repetitive spinning chorus of the women.

Erik, for his part, is a relic from the Romantic opera Wagner is beginning to cast aside like a shedding skin. He even seems like a tenor who has unfortunately wandered into the wrong work. But for all his ordinariness, Erik is given a certain dignity in his final aria recalling the good times with Senta. Incidentally, the lyricism he represents—and that also underlies the Dutchman's duet with Senta—is a striking testimony to the love of bel canto opera, Italian style, that Wagner absorbed during his many years as a young conductor of repertory opera. The Italianate influence adds yet another fascinating texture to this early masterpiece.

Yet the contrast Erik's sunny but predictable nature presents (as a foil to the Dutchman) leads to one of those knotty dramaturgical problems that crop up constantly in Wagner's work. It is precisely the sympathetic portrait of Erik that temps the audience to linger in the moment. But this would distract from Wagner's overall design. Erik is thus rudely cast aside from the action. These speed bumps are headaches for stage directors (or, sometimes, the inspiration to brilliant solutions). For Wagner himself, the most typical solution is found in the intensity of the music. With the final entrance of the Dutchman, the score's temperature heats up, urging beyond the immediate dramatic situation to the heart of the matter, which is how the Dutchman is to escape his curse now that the pattern of disappointment seems to be recurring. Erik's untimely—indeed, unlikely—disappearance is immediately overshadowed.

The overture (CD 1, track 1) gives a strong dose of this intensity from the onset. Wagner composed it last, after completing the basic outlines of the score in an inspired frenzy of seven weeks (even in his much longer scores, he often worked fast during the first stage of his composition process). It neatly synthesizes the chief musical features of the opera to come into a kind of prefiguring drama-in-miniature. Wagner takes a cue from Beethoven in the hollow sound of the stings' tremolo open fifths heard in the very first measure (0:01). This chord has an indeterminacy—lacking the complete triad, it could turn either major or minor—that makes the opening of Beethoven's Ninth Symphony resemble a cloud of chaos from which order must emerge. Wagner had been overwhelmed by a powerful performance of the Ninth in Paris (in those days, such events were still a rarity), and Beethoven's symphonies remained critical touchstones for him. Almost immediately, the theme associated with the Dutchman is declared by horns (0:03) and then echoed by a fierce battery of the entire brass (0:12).

But one can already sense an important difference between Wagner and Beethoven. Beethoven's Ninth, for example, introduces a theme that can be easily broken into constituent parts to be examined and then recombined, opening up a whole world of guises and evolving identities. Wagner's theme is simple and basic (built simply from spelling out the strings' "hollow chord" of the opening) but has a completeness that makes it readily identifiable. The boldness of its upward thrust, together with the instrumental coloring of the brass instruments, gives it, in other words, a musical characterization. Add the churning of the sea Wagner suggests in his manic string figurations (3:09), and a memorable musical depiction of the Dutchman's restless striving becomes fixed in the mind. Wagner eventually introduces a highly contrasting theme in F major (1:26).

This melody, associated with Senta, at first seems to offer "classical" contrast, with its shy, lilting descent and plangent scoring for woodwinds. But even its shape is driven by dramatic as much as musical aspects. As the woman who will redeem the

Dutchman, Senta inspires music that at first calms and counter-balances the ascending thrust and striving of the cursed sailor. Yet she also joins his world, and her music too eventually winds its way upward in a kind of expectant, sympathetic echo (1:34). This theme intermittently breaks in (e.g., 6:50) to calm the agitated music surrounding it in the overture.

Wagner's scene-painting of stormy seas here is justly cele-brated. It's an early paradigm of his expertise at finding musical equivalents for the most elemental forces of nature—a facility that often colors his scores, above all in the *Ring*. At the same time, the stormy weather one seems to hear isn't just literal but a powerful depiction of the Dutchman's interior world, his very consciousness. In this context, the soothing effect of Senta's music becomes even more meaningful.

As the seas roil and pitch in the score, Wagner already demonstrates an early and remarkable ability to control the emotional flexibility of expression in a way that suggests some-thing beyond the music itself. He manipulates agitation and passing calm as indicators of the Dutchman's frustrated search for peace. A wonderful example occurs in the final moments, when he amps up the excitement in a fanfarelike outburst and a last, blazing restatement of the Dutchman's theme (now firmly anchored in major-key harmonies) (9:02). To this Wagner now appends a serene closure (9:26). The volume subsides and, against a counterpart of harp arpeggios and Senta's melody in the winds, a new theme soars in the violins (9:35).

Some might recognize this motive from the last movement of the "Jupiter" Symphony, which Mozart, like Wagner here, borrowed from a well-known church cadence. The resolution isn't entirely convincing. Indeed it has an air of being tacked on—which in fact it was, during one of the numerous revisions Wagner subsequently made to the score. But it is significant as a musical marker for one of those ideas beyond the music that are essential to understanding the work as a whole. With its resolution of the music onto a different plane that is by implication spiritual (the church cadence), this section points ahead to the dramatic action of redemption. In fact, it's the place where one really senses that redemption occurs (when Wagner repeats this passage at the opera's conclusion). In Wagner's personal philosophy, this redemption must be brought about through the reality of a woman's love. And already here, as demonstrated by the strange Senta, this is a far cry from the ordinary love of romantic effusiveness. Just what form this love should take, and how it can be grasped, will continue to preoccupy Wagner throughout the rest of his creative life.

What Kind of Love To Sing?

Tannhäuser

Tannhäuser was a problem child for Wagner. The widely held image of the composer as an unbendably haughty figure maintaining airs of artistic infallibility is belied by a number of self-confessed creative struggles throughout his career—nowhere more so than in *Tannhäuser.* Wagner recognized *Der fliegende Holländer,* for example, as the breakthrough that first introduced his authentic voice. But he was hardly averse to revising that score: both for practical reasons (in cleaning up the orchestration) and, later, to clarify the role played by redemptive love in the new musical coda he appended. Yet he went to unusual pains when it came to sizing up *Tannhäuser,* adding (and also cutting) music and text but never quite solving the matter to his satisfaction. The process began immediately after *Tannhäuser*'s lukewarm premiere in Dresden in October 1845; it continued right up to the last year of the composer's life, when his second wife Cosima noted that he felt he "still owed the world" his *Tannhäuser.* No other work from the Wagner canon shares quite this sense of being—at least from the composer's point of view—"unfinished."

But *Tannhäuser* quickly recovered from its inauspicious unveiling. During the following few decades, it established itself (in tandem with *Lohengrin,* which eventually eclipsed it) as the best-known, best-loved Wagner opera among the

general public. It's a curious fact that this work, which continues to blend elements of the old with the new, represented
what many of his contemporaries meant when they referred to
the "Wagnerian" approach, far removed as it is from the truly
novel artwork of the future that we think of as the quintes-
sential Wagner.

The poet Charles Baudelaire penned an influential essay in
praise of the opera's "intoxicating" beauty that helped solidify
the composer's standing for a whole generation of French artists. And shortly after the first version of *Tannhäuser* had been
premiered in 1845, a young man wrote a lengthy essay launch-
ing his career as perhaps the most important music critic of
the latter half of the nineteenth century. This was Eduard
Hanslick—later perceived as Wagner's arch-enemy in the critical establishment—who found *Tannhäuser* proof that its creator
should be considered "the greatest dramatic talent among all
contemporary composers."

Wagner had much at stake with *Tannhäuser*. He was desperately eager for a follow-up to the success that finally had come
his way with *Rienzi*. The latter's triumphant premiere increased
Wagner's confidence, but now he desired success on his own
terms, with an opera in which his inner world was more intimately invested. *Der fliegende Holländer* had been given a disap-
pointing reception (largely on account of its uneven casting).
And for all of Wagner's self-identification with the Dutchman's
alienated state, he was basically glorifying a popular spooky
tale into the status of myth. In contrast, the subject matter of
Tannhäuser opened up a rich world of truly mythic resonance
that seemed inexhaustible and would provide enough material
for his entire creative life.

The process began during Wagner's down-and-out days in
Paris, when he took refuge with a trio of close friends. This
group of artistically inclined German expatriates could have

come straight out of Puccini's *La Bohème.* One of these was Samuel Lehrs, a classical philologist, young, deeply impoverished, and tragically ill, who averted Wagner's attention to the possibilities of medieval legend and mythology: in particular, some of the sources that would stimulate Wagner's interest in the figures of Tannhäuser and Lohengrin.

After he had given up on Paris in 1842, Wagner recalled a memorable experience during the journey back to Dresden, his home for the next seven years. Off in the distance but imposing, he caught sight of the legendary castle of the Wartburg in Thuringia (where, as part of a long litany of its historical lore, Martin Luther had once taken refuge). The impression was strong enough that it inspired him to incorporate the castle and its valley into *Tannhäuser,* thus endowing the opera with a highly specific location (a trait shared among the canonical works only by *Die Meistersinger*). In his last letter to Lehrs in April 1843, the composer, poignantly unaware that his friend would prematurely die in a matter of days, mentions the recent completion of his *Tannhäuser* libretto and promises to send it with his next correspondence, as if in token of a dream that had been shared by the group of close-knit friends finally coming to pass.

Once Wagner had returned from Paris, he really did seem ready to make it with his new Dresden appointment. The success of *Rienzi* encouraged him and his wife Minna (together with the pets the animal-loving Wagner could not live without) to move into upscale lodgings with a view of the elegant Zwinger Palace. Typically, he was already beginning to live beyond his means, but he had a lot of lost time to make up for from his Parisian penury. *Tannhäuser* was thus the first work Wagner composed, in relative calm, after returning from his long self-imposed exile (which foreshadowed an even longer exile to come). At last he had opened the door to the fame and eager public he lusted after with his *Rienzi,* a work that proved he could successfully cater to the expectations for fashionable grand opera. Now the ambitious thirty-year-old Kapellmeister was more determined than ever to make his mark with what truly moved *him* (notwithstanding the disappointment of his Dutchman). His new project hit upon what he believed represented his "most original creation" up to that point.

Wagner drew on a motley collection of sources: the writings of such German romantics as Tieck, Hoffmann, and Heine, but more significantly the medieval legends with which Samuel Lehrs had made him familiar. In what would become Wagner's signature treatment of such material, he wove two originally separate and wholly unrelated strands together into one interlocking story. These involved, first, the morality tale about a knight (known by the name of the town whence he originates) from the era of the Crusades who had indulged his senses in the underground domain of Venus. This is where medieval topography located the pagan gods, imagined to have been banished by Christianity. The knight eventually fled and sought repentance but was told that only when the Pope's staff of wood put forth green leaves would he be saved (in the original folk version, the miracle happens too late, only after Tannhäuser has returned in despair to the clutches of Venus). The other strand (which provides the basis for act 2 of Wagner's opera) centered around the culture of the medieval minnesingers, the minstrels of chivalric love who competed in jousts not of arms but of art. The two strands are merged in the opera's full title: *Tannhäuser und der Sängerkrieg auf Wartburg* (Tannhäuser and the Song Contest on the Wartburg). This is a theme Wagner will reintroduce in his comic work from the 1860s, *Die Meistersinger*. In fact, he originally conceived the latter as a lighter companion piece, in the mold of a classical Greek *satyr play* (the shorter, parodistic plays performed as comic relief at the great tragic festivals) to set beside the "romantic tragedy" of *Tannhäuser*.

Actually there's a third strand, embodied in the character of Elisabeth, the counterpart to Venus. She is Wagner's synthetic creation of a heroine, drawn from multiple sources. And she fulfills multiple—and to an important extent, contradictory—functions in her role as the opera's agent of salvation. Referred to but unseen in act 1, Elisabeth is the archetypal virginal object of chivalric desire. The mere mention of her anchors the confused Tannhäuser's determination to return to the society of the Wartburg. In act 2, she is the prize who presides over the song contest and reciprocates with her own humanly expressed desire for Tannhäuser. Yet the final act presents her refracted through the figure of the legendary St. Elisabeth of Hungary, an early adherent of the revolutionary, humble, poverty-embracing Franciscan order. Her intercession for Tannhäuser proves her efficacy in channeling the redemptive force. She wields the true power—the Pope's blossoming staff is only a confirming symbol of it (rather like Wagner's recasting of the love potion in *Tristan*).

What is characteristically Wagnerian in all this is the appropriation of external sources to encode an intensely internal struggle. Wagner uses a medieval setting (mingled too with the classical echoes of Venus, here a Circe-like figure) as a guise to grapple with what he feels are urgent issues of modernity—or rather, of timeless, existential validity. Even his unusually specific setting of the Wartburg does not limit him to a historically picturesque bit of local color. Rather, it serves as a familiar backdrop, providing the necessary aura for the emotional warfare that is waged alongside the artistic battles in *Tannhäuser*.

Bolder still is Wagner's appropriation of traditional religious symbolism and content in the service of an artistic vision. Aside from the anticlerical clichés of *Rienzi* and hazy references in *Der fliegende Holländer* to damnation and saving angels, *Tannhäuser* is the first of his works to employ this strategy seriously. It will

reach its controversial climax in his final music drama, *Parsifal*.
A measure of how effectively Wagner establishes an atmosphere of medieval Catholicism in *Tannhäuser* (especially in the
last act and its dramatization of repentance) might be seen in
the rumors later recounted by the composer that he had been
bribed "by Catholic interests" to write the opera. More significantly, Wagner (at the time an avowed atheist) scorned the
absurdity of critics "who insist on reading into my *Tannhäuser* a
specifically Christian and pietistic drift."

The opera is still—astonishingly, in spite of the evidence
contained in the music—sometimes dismissed as a prim fable
from Victorian times, with no possible relation to our own.
The mistake (as among Wagner's original misinterpreters) is to
take at face value, in traditional terms, the oppositions that permeate *Tannhäuser*: the Venusberg vs. the Wartburg, paganism
vs. Christianity, flesh vs. spirit, anarchy vs. decorum, nature vs.
civilization, orgiastic desire vs. chivalric love, eros vs. agape,
arrogance vs. repentance. Yet Wagner is hardly interested
merely in replicating the burden of an old morality tale with its
preordained conclusion. We have already witnessed how he sets
up the elemental polarity in *Der fliegende Holländer*—between
restless striving and the desire for peace—in a way that renders
the stakes of the drama extreme. Such dualisms provide Wagner
a plane on which to enact humanity's fundamental struggles,
particularly when they are internalized within the same character. Even more to the point, their very exaggeration of contrast
engenders a potential for vivid musical expression; this in turn
allows for more intense identification from the audience.

Clearly one of the first aspects of the *Tannhäuser* legend to
attract Wagner was its suitability for evoking wildly differentiated but coexisting sound worlds. The familiar overture
recapitulates these contrasts in advance. Choralelike progres-
sions in the "Pilgrim's Chorus" connote the steadfast assurance

of faith. But they frame a statement of anxious longing in the strings against shifting, uncertain harmonies. Following one of Wagner's favorite devices, a long, steady crescendo to climax and then an abbreviated diminuendo, the audience enters the domain of Venus. It entices with an array of quivering tremolos, surging rhythms, and dizzying chromaticism, all deployed to bewitching effect within a general context of E major (a key that the composer associated with magic and enchantment). This is the same key characterizing Mendelssohn's elfin *Midsummer Night's Dream* music, a contemporaneous score whose indelible (but unacknowledged) influence on Wagner can be discerned here.

The siren sounds of the Venusberg were how Wagner had first worked his way musically into the world of *Tannhäuser*. Later he recognized the opera's opening scene as its weakest spot. Ironically, Wagner prepared a major overhaul of the opera in 1861 for a Paris revival—for the very city, that is, from which he had fled to be able to write just such a work in peace. This is known, from its later published form, as the "Paris version," in contrast to the "Dresden version," which is largely based on the original 1845 production in Dresden. The occasion was a command performance by Napoleon III for the Paris Opera (by then *Tannhäuser*'s popularity had already been established). After an extraordinary amount of effort in preparing this new version, it ended up as one of opera's legendary fiascos for extramusical reasons. Wagner had provided a lengthier ballet to suit Parisian taste—but in the first scene, where it made dramatic sense, and not, as was customary, in the second act. This gave Wagner's opponents only another excuse to savage a production they had already decided to disrupt for political reasons. The composer withdrew the opera after a miserable three performances.

But he chose the Paris version to supersede its Dresden precursor. What is particularly striking about the former is its extensive rewriting of the Venusberg scenes. By 1861 Wagner had given birth to his pioneering *Tristan und Isolde,* and he drew on the new perspective he had achieved there, in both its musical and philosophical exploration of desire, to breathe fresh life into Tannhäuser's sojourn with Venus. He cropped the overture's final recapitulation (which had rounded out a traditional ABA form) to segue into a lengthier section of musical scene-painting as a setup for the ballet. When detached from its context, this music for Venus's realm of the senses, with its satyrs, fauns, nymphs, and bacchantes engaged in orgiastic frenzy, seems like a peculiarly garish din but aptly establishes the atmosphere.

And that atmosphere, as it unfolds, is marvelously variegated and not exactly predictable. The Venusberg is a place of erotic extremes, of fantasies lived out—a metaphor too, perhaps, of the realm of pure, mindless entertainment Wagner felt the opera world of his time glorified. It exudes dystopian decadence and is the X-rated zone of the work. This is where Tannhäuser reaches his nadir of ennui. Satiety cancels out longing, and his only hope, like Faust's refusal to linger, is to return from this repetitive bacchanalia to the human realm of change. Yet the Venusberg also entails elements of a utopian Hellenic beauty. Particularly in Wagner's more expansive Paris portrayal of Venus, with its suppler vocal lines, the goddess emerges as a fully rounded figure who not only offers unlimited pleasure but also nurtures Tannhäuser and fears his return to "the cold world of men." From Wagner's post-*Tristan* stance, her association with the realm of night contains a dramatic truth that goes beyond a lust-satisfying sexpot. This is something the composer had already intuited in a description of Venus he penned in 1851 as inhabiting the "realm of non-being," which is actually *beyond* desire and its satisfaction. Tannhäuser's way to salvation, it turns out, is to play a kind of Orpheus-in-reverse, who retreats from the underworld and is reconnected with the woman he has abandoned in the land of the living.

One of the opera's most powerful scenes, indeed, is the transformation of the Venusberg into the valley above as Tannhäuser encounters the world of simple, unadorned nature again after his dalliance in Venus's false, artificial utopia of the senses. As Wagner later develops his art, such transition scenes—and the connections they create between disparate aspects within a work—come increasingly to the fore. They reach their consummation in the overwhelming music of the two "transformation" scenes Wagner wrote for *Parsifal*. Certain productions make a lot of mileage out of highlighting such connections in *Tannhäuser* to give some depth to the opera's more obviously schematic framework. An especially memorable example is the beautifully conceived simplicity of Werner Herzog's production from the late 1990s: billowing red silk representing the Venusberg is abruptly pulled offstage to unveil the green valley where Tannhäuser begins to make his painful transition back to humanity.

The middle act, above all, is where we sense Wagner still inhabiting the world of old-fashioned opera, with its subdividable set pieces: arias, a duet, a stately march, and a climactic septet with chorus. The composer's idiom is more conservative here than in several sections of the outer acts. In a sense, though, this merely replicates the experience of Tannhäuser's own temporary return from a realm of absolute freedom to the more formal society he had rejected. And anyone who doubts Wagner's ability to craft an outright beautiful aria will lose the argument when listening to the music that opens this act, "Dich, teure Halle" ("Beloved Hall, I greet you") (CD 1, track 2). This first appearance of Elisabeth is in the form of a traditional *apostrophe aria* (a direct address to an object, in this case the Wartburg's song contest hall that she is entering again for the first time since Tannhäuser's absence). It illuminates Wagner's mastery of voice-centered lyricism.

At the same time, with its own more delicately traced chromaticism, it creates a vivid portrait that intriguingly complements our now firmly established image of Venus. In the mold of virtually all of Wagner's future heroines, Elisabeth stands for multiple personalities rolled into one. Rather than the saintly figure who emerges in the final act, Elisabeth is presented in this aria as a woman with very human desires. An unmistakable sexual urgency inflects the rhythmic excitement of this music, with its rapid-fire pulses (0:40 ff) and toppling syncopations (0:32). Meanwhile, in the slower, melancholy middle section (1:18 ff), Elisabeth's lost joie de vivre acts as a kind of sympathetic echo for Tannhäuser (much like Senta's rapport with the Dutchman). The aria's climactic exuberance (3:18) instills a sense of confidence that counterbalances Venus's parting curse. It even foreshadows the ecstatic outburst of Tannhäuser's song, that arrogant throwing of the gauntlet before the society into which he had thought he could be reintegrated.

Wagner's inspiration, unfortunately, does not rise to the occasion for the central song contest—even in the Paris version, where he made the exchange tauter and intensified the music signaling Tannhäuser's sudden possession by memories of Venus. Perhaps the basic flaw here is that his friend Wolfram's serene interlude lacks a strong profile to differentiate it dramatically from the aggressively defiant lyricism of Tannhäuser's ode (already heard three times, at progressive pitch levels, in the Venusberg scene). As in Plato's *Symposium,* the topic of the contest is to describe the nature of love: the real question that is at the heart of *Tannhäuser.* The hero's enthusiastic paean to Venus meets a shrill interruption (it prefigures the catastrophic intrusion on Tristan's night scene with Isolde). The way the contest plays out leaves the audience with a feeling of incompletion, of the question left not fully answered—rather like Wagner's own unease with giving closure to the opera even after numerous revisions.

Revealingly, Tannhäuser's antithesis to the love described by Wolfram, which so shocks his audience and precipitates the final conflict, is invoked from heartfelt experience, not from idealism. Tannhäuser's outburst, with its flower-power, seize-the-day candor, in fact serves to demystify the kind of reverential love epitomized in Wolfram's chivalric verses. And as is known from the composer's own statements in letters and elsewhere, this proto-Freudian point of view is one with which Wagner had great sympathy.

Yet this too is only part of the whole picture. Wagner's musical strength resumes for the great turning point of the opera, as Elisabeth's plea interrupts the massed anger of the community and Tannhäuser embarks on his journey of repentance and withdrawal. The prelude to act 3 (which Wagner labels "Tannhäuser's Pilgrimage") recapitulates the hero's internal transformation more movingly—and efficiently—than the drama by itself could. Its counterpart is Tannhäuser's lengthy "Rome Narrative," a monologue recounting the story of the Pope's apparent inability to accept his repentance. In contrast with Elisabeth's arias, this is the opera's most celebrated moment of looking ahead musically to the intensified, freer declamation that will become a hallmark of the artwork of the future.

It consolidates the sense of alienation Wagner had first explored in the Dutchman's comparable "Die Frist ist um" but takes it to a further extreme, both dramatically and musically. Tannhäuser's conclusion that redemption is unavailable to him is made all the bitterer by the brief glimmer of hope he had allowed. And like *Der fliegende Holländer*, *Tannhäuser* contains no actual villains. The source of unhappiness and suffering for both protagonists is an inevitable and crucial aspect of life itself as they must live it.

Who then *is* Tannhäuser? He is undeniably a portrait of the artist. Yet in his repentance, he is forced to deny the very uniqueness that characterizes his art. Like the Dutchman, he is a wanderer: but of his own choosing, not as a result of the unfaithfulness of others. Tannhäuser is an outsider, cursed by his very desire to embrace what life offers—cursed, that is, always to seek beyond what he is given. Perhaps Wagner found him too close to home to establish the distance he needed to imagine a more fully rounded music for his hero. Tannhäuser's extremity of longing is, as Wagner encapsulates it, for "the highest form of love." Yet his inability himself to grasp what he has experienced, through both Venus and Elisabeth (sometimes, in high-concept productions, played by the same performer), weakens our sense of a positive, fully integrated conclusion. Wagner's notorious awkwardness with endings is at its most obvious here. The deaths of Elisabeth and Tannhäuser are dramatically unsatisfying, for they feel too schematic. So Wagner relies on his score to do this work for us. In an essay in *First Intermissions* from his Metropolitan Opera broadcasts, the sharply perceptive M. Owen Lee observes that "just as the papal staff has sprouted leaves, so Wagner's Christian hymn, the 'Pilgrim's Chorus,' is surrounded at the close by the pulsing music of paganism (the frenzied broken triplets from the Venusberg)." As in the conclusion to *Der fliegende Holländer,* it's the musical symbolism that is left to carry the weight of tying up loose ends. Wagner will find progressively more sophisticated means to accomplish such endings as his art matures.

Making Contact
The Tragedy of *Lohengrin*

L ohengrin is the saddest of Wagner's creations. Elsewhere, to be sure, he depicts more harrowing agonies of despair, plumbs far deeper levels of suffering. But with his idiosyncratic reworking of the tale of the Swan Knight, Wagner gives voice to a beautiful hope, only to show its inevitable disappointment. *Lohengrin* draws on what up to now had obsessed Wagner as an artist, but it treats these concerns with a more finely integrated clarity, in both dramatic and musical terms. Its psychological complexity draws us in more closely than the schematic shortcuts of *Tannhäuser*. And while Wagner did not realize it at the time, the opera marks a significant turning point in his career. Here his youthful search for artistic validation reaches its pinnacle and sets him free for the radical departure to come.

Wagner worried that once *Tannhäuser* was completed, he would be unable to find material of comparable resonance to fire his inspiration. His earlier dalliance with medieval German sources back in the Paris days had already made him well aware of the Lohengrin legend. But his enchantment was not instant. Wagner scornfully observed that "the medieval poem which has preserved this highly poetical legend contains the most inadequate and pedestrian account to have come down to us." Even more to the point, he noted that "the medieval poem

presented Lohengrin in a mystic twilight that filled me with suspicion." The knight appears in the Grail epics of Wolfram von
Eschenbach (the same Wolfram whom Wagner introduced as
one of Tannhäuser's fellow minnesingers) and is also the subject
of an anonymous epic. Wagner had brought this material along
with him to the water-cure resort of Marienbad in Bohemia,
where he spent the summer of 1845 recuperating after he had
wrapped up *Tannhäuser* and the recent Dresden season.

Yet that summer the figure at last began to percolate in
his imagination. Wagner was rewarded with one of his great
"eureka moments" (in some accounts insistently leaping out
of the healing mineral waters, against doctor's orders, to
sketch out a prose draft). By now the pattern is a familiar one:
Wagner's fascination comes alive as soon as he is able to project
an internal connection onto his source. The sudden, instinc-
tive discovery of relevance for his personal unhappiness and
(by implication) for contemporary society triggers a sense of
creative urgency. His enthusiasm sets in motion a process of
synthesizing everything that seems vital to the issue at hand.
Often this is by grafting together disparate sources; but it's also
by homing in on the essentials—as in the case of the Lohengrin
tale, once he had "learned it in its simplest outlines."

Wagner meanwhile continued his musical duties at the
Dresden Royal Court Theatre, working on his new opera over
the next two and a half years whenever he could steal time
away. His position as Kapellmeister was becoming a source of
increasing frustration. Wagner's attempts to spur some kind
of serious institutional reform continued to run up against the
intransigence of his superiors. (Wagner was, incidentally, an
extremely influential conductor in his own time. His philosophy
of performance centered on a flexible idea of tempo intended
to foreground the "melody"—that is, all the elements involved
in a score's essential expression. This approach became the

template for an entire school of conducting based on interpretive empathy, which continues in full swing today. At the other extreme was the finesse and dedication to precision championed by Mendelssohn.) Concentration on *Lohengrin,* the full score of which he completed in April 1848, served as both a means of escape and a creative outlet to express his preoccupation with an artistic utopia. Wagner later recalled the time actually devoted to its composition as an exceptionally fertile and satisfying period.

Simultaneously, the political unrest that had been stirring throughout Europe was coming to a boil. Wagner regarded the revolutionaries' struggle as a natural extension of the goals he sought through artistic revolution to free society from an oppressive old order it had inherited. He began to espouse radical political ideas acquired from Proudhon and the socialists, such as the elimination of property. He eagerly joined their cause when the uprising came to Dresden in 1849. But the long-awaited utopia did not arrive. When the Prussian army quashed the rebellion, Wagner's "mug-sketch" was posted next to his arrest warrant "for taking part in riots." The artist-turned-political-fugitive escaped by the skin of his teeth. He retreated for a time to Paris and then began a long exile from German soil, making Switzerland his new home. Plans for the premiere of his new opera in Dresden had meanwhile been disrupted by the Revolution. Wagner's artistic ally Franz Liszt was entrusted with *Lohengrin*'s first performance, which was given—in the composer's absence—in August 1850 in Weimar, with an absurdly inadequate orchestra of just thirty-eight players. The premiere was not a success. From his new perch in Switzerland, Wagner would lament how his inability to hear his own music performed brought him closer to understanding what the experience of deafness must have been like for Beethoven.

Eventually, *Lohengrin* would emerge as the most popular Wagner opera of the nineteenth century. If *Tannhäuser* was misread by some of Wagner's more literal-minded contemporaries as a piety-affirming spectacle, *Lohengrin*'s aura of medieval fantasy would invite a whole spectrum of misguided appropriations. On one extreme was the type of innocuous, romanticizing nostalgia for a vanished time exemplified by King Ludwig II of Bavaria. His devotion to the work and self-identification with the knight were extreme. This future patron of the composer, overwhelmingly swept away into Wagner's world when he first saw *Lohengrin,* went over the top to commemorate his passion. The result was his fairy-tale castle at Neuschwanstein, the model for the Disney Cinderella's Castle. On the other, ominous extreme, Hitler hijacked the theme of a knightly hero's glorious apparition in a time of need as an allegory for Germany's destiny to accept the services of its miraculous Führer (remaining oblivious, as he was in the case of the *Ring,* to the opera's actual denouement).

To be sure, the tale of *Lohengrin* is replete with a host of iconic images from Romanticism's fascination with the Middle Ages: the knight's silvery approach in a swan-drawn skiff; the innocent damsel in distress, rescued by her longed-for suitor in a trial-by-combat; references to the Holy Grail; and so on. But Wagner's stance clearly anticipates the idea of the collective unconscious later articulated by Carl Jung, as well as Joseph Campbell's comparative mythology. In his various elaborations on the opera's poetic message, Wagner discounts the medieval religious trappings of the figure. These result, he believes, merely from Christianity's desire to shape legends inherited from immemorial wisdom according to its specific biases. The tale's origin predates "the Christian's bent toward supernaturalism," instead arising "from the truest depths of universal human nature." Wagner hearkens back to Greek mythology to draw parallels. Just as the Flying Dutchman and Tannhäuser are variants on the Hellenic prototype of Odysseus (as wanderer and as an adventurer waylaid by the seductions of Circe), the encounter between Lohengrin and Elsa has its counterpart in the myth of Zeus and Semele (which, rather than the story of Cupid and Psyche, seems to have drawn his attention). Wagner summarizes the significance of this core myth in terms of what it tells us about the "inmost essence" of human nature, which centers on *"the necessity of love."* He continues:

> [T]he essence of this love, in its truest utterance, is the *longing for utmost physical reality,* for fruition in an object that can be grasped by all the senses, held fast with all the force of actual being. In this finite, physically sure embrace, must not the god dissolve and disappear? Is not the mortal, who had yearned for god, undone, annulled? Yet is not love, in its truest, highest essence, herein revealed?

What is extraordinary here is Wagner's focus on what film directors think of as multiple points of view. His capacity to envision the story as unfolding in a mutual process for his characters opens up a richer dimension. Elsa isn't the only one seeking salvation, nor is she the sole victim when she succumbs to asking the forbidden question. The crux of the myth, as Wagner perceives it, is the *mirroring* that happens between both: Lohengrin too hopes to find redemption through Elsa and in turn is destroyed. All too briefly, both seem to find what they had longed for in each other. But the happiness has no chance to last—not only because Elsa cannot reasonably be expected to suppress her natural (although manipulated) curiosity, but because Lohengrin's desire for unconditional love is paradoxically framed by his condition that she never ask him his name and origin.

In this meeting between two of humanity's fundamental impulses—toward transcendence and concrete understanding on the one hand and experience in the here-and-now on the other—Wagner finds an irreconcilable conflict of interest. To express its true significance is the task of music, which serves "to complement the meaning" only hinted at in the drama. He describes this tension elsewhere as the "contact between a metaphysical phenomenon and human nature, and the impossibility that such contact will last." As we saw in his first complete opera, *Die Feen,* Wagner had long been attracted to the mythic potential of love stories between humans and supernatural figures. *Der fliegende Holländer* and *Tannhäuser* sharpen the encounter to a pattern of interplay between disappointment in the pattern of existence and hope; the unexpected triumph of hope is effected only by extreme dramatic crisis. In *Lohengrin,* Wagner's outlook clearly darkens. This "contact" between the utopian and the actual gives shape to our deepest longings: for love that lasts, for an ideal society. But the gap between them can never be bridged.

Wagner took great care in preparing his poetic text and was particularly pleased with how it turned out. Indeed, in its elaboration of the characters' inner motivations and structuring, the libretto stands out as one of his finest. His subtler shifts in perspective create a space wherein the music can operate more fully and with deeper internal coherence. Take the opening scene of the opera, which establishes the setting as tenth-century Brabant, near Antwerp. The wise King Henry the Fowler has come from the neighboring German lands to seek help against invading forces and is disturbed by the social unrest that greets him. Is Wagner suddenly reverting to the fashionable genre of historical opera that he had decided was a dead end after *Rienzi?* Wagner scholar Carl Dahlhaus, in his *Richard Wagner's Music Dramas,* suggests that *Lohengrin* synthesizes

elements from the genres of myth, history, fairy tale, and tragedy. He sees the purpose of the history-slanted exposition and
framing as a means to foreground the heart of the matter, which
is the Lohengrin-Elsa encounter. The historical setting intersects with the fairy-tale aspect of the latter and thus amplifies
Lohengrin's underlying tension between the real and the ideal.

Thus, Wagner opens by depicting a society gone awry.
But through the course of this neatly paced, economical act,
he shifts to the isolated perspective of Elsa, falsely accused
of murdering her brother, then to the sudden appearance of
Lohengrin and his even more sudden (but condition-bound)
love for her. He then returns to the surrounding society that
celebrates his triumph. (A somewhat similar strategy, although
in the opposite direction, might be noted in *King Lear*. There, a
fairy-tale-like opening is followed by the more realistic plot of
a brother's resentment, with the two eventually intertwining.)
Even more, this contrast between genres—the historical and
the fairy tale—allows Wagner to reinforce his musical contrasts
to marvelous and suggestive effect. The now-familiar polarities that stimulate the composer's musical imagination take on
greater nuance.

The maximum contrast is, of course, between the worldly,
muscular, fanfare-driven music of the social context of Brabant
and the glowing serenity Lohengrin imports from the Grail. But
the latter is introduced (apart from the prelude) only as Elsa
recounts her dream. Her sound world, with its characteristic
melancholy relegated to the woodwinds, acts as a more anxious
counterpart to Lohengrin's music. The themes directly associated with the knight reveal an assertive, extroverted character
(e.g., CD 1, track 4, 4:42) more aligned with the muscular
sounds of the fanfares than with the Grail's gentle poetry.
Against all of this, an especially thrilling—and musically

forward-looking—dimension appears in the dark strains of the villains Ortrud and Telramund as their counterplot unfolds.

Intriguingly, the opera's celebrated prelude (CD 1, track 3) dispenses with such contrasts. Its sound world marks an extraordinary leap forward in Wagner's art. His previous overtures were basically of the conventional "potpourri" type: a gathering place and sneak preview of the chief musical themes to unfold in the coming drama. The strategy in *Lohengrin* is quite different. Wagner immediately establishes the otherworldly atmosphere of the Grail with which the hero is associated (0:01) and sustains this mood throughout. The material is essentially monothematic (although subtly intertwined with aspects of Elsa's related music in the major-to-minor shifts [e.g., 2:46]), based on a theme of long-held notes alternating with dotted ones (0:23).

Monothematic but not monotonous: the marvel here is how Wagner plays stasis against movement. The effect has been described as a kind of "hovering" but might also be compared to light through stained glass. Yet even without the tension contrasting material would generate, he creates a sense of subtle, iridescent shifting as the music progresses. The prelude metaphorically descends through the orchestra with a carefully gauged gravitational pull, as one can hear when a new zone of textures is introduced in lower registers (e.g., 1:55). At the same time, Wagner unfurls a vast, slow-motion crescendo extending up to the prelude's brassy climax (5:19) and then reverses course for a gently tapered diminuendo (6:09) to a gently falling scalar melody and a briefer ascent (7:19) back into the heights.

Wagner achieves all of this with a newfound painterly approach to his large array of instrumental forces. Clearly one of the great payoffs of his day-to-day ennui as Kapellmeister was the confidence in the art of orchestration he gained from the job. The prelude's opening measures offer a microcosm: chords blend in the flutes, oboes, and violins. Extremely detailed instructions divide the last into separate groups with multiple solo parts (played with a bowing technique to produce *harmonics,* which ethereally project the higher overtones contained within a pitch). The resulting sound of this total mix has a numinous quality and seems to shimmer from within. Thomas Mann raptly compared it to a "silver-blue." An echo too can perhaps be heard in the beginning of the slow movement of Mahler's Fourth Symphony, which the composer, drawn to the same end of the spectrum in his own color metaphor, described as "the undifferentiated blue" of the sky.

The subtler use of musical polarities in *Lohengrin* further demonstrates Wagner's artistic advance. Previously, he markedly delineated the sound worlds dividing the Dutchman from Senta and, even more, their internal space from the mundane world. The Wartburg and the ensemble of pilgrims likewise inhabit a musical space keenly contrasted with the Venusberg's chromatic pleasures. Like Senta, Elsa dreams of her obsession before the knight appears to her in reality. But her music has subtle affinities with that of the Grail and of Lohengrin. Even her signature key of A-flat, as has been frequently noted, lies next to the Grail's emblematic A major, a literal half-step *descent* from its luminous aura. Meanwhile, the characters of Ortrud and Telramund establish yet another musical antipode. Yet Ortrud's defining F-sharp minor is in fact intertwined with the Grail as relative minor to its A major—much as her pagan character is the natural obverse of the knight's idealism. In a sense, her subplot—enacting the pagan desire for revenge against an encroaching religion—ironically confirms Wagner's observation (quoted above) about the Christian co-opting of inherited myths. But *Lohengrin's* repeated opposition of *Zauber* (magic) and *Wunder* (miracle) isn't merely a theatrical effect.

It's an integral motive, for in Elsa these two forces meet up to confront each other as her doubt takes root.

Act 2 gives the spotlight to Ortrud's point of view. The proportions of this act, interestingly, are longer relative to the outer acts than anywhere else in Wagner (aside from *Die Walküre*). He saved this music for last when working out the score's fuller details, having begun with act 3. And the actual sound world in the prelude and masterful first scene of act 2 is already within earshot of some of the most thrilling moments yet to be born in the *Ring*. Wagner had already mastered a way to depict elemental forces that are amoral (the sea, desire). This is his first serious depiction of evil. Wagner gives musical substance to the Zauber of Ortrud's realm as a form of hate. In a letter to Liszt, he comments on Ortrud's character as a woman who can feel only one love: "love of the past, of departed generations, the dreadfully insane love of ancestral pride which can express itself only as hatred towards all that lives, all that really exists."

Wagner brings this evil to the stage with a music of brooding intensity that hereafter is often closely associated with the powers of destruction. In both dramaturgical and musical terms, he has already entered a realm entirely apart from the boilerplate stage villain who is conjured with a kit of hackneyed devices. Ortrud has a truly Shakespearean resonance—many consider her scenes the most powerful Wagner had written up to this point. Even his instrumentation of her chthonic music is like a negative reflection of the Grail's upward-floating phrases. It plunges instead into the registral depths, making the most of shadowy lower strings and winds. Ortrud's main theme itself takes an unstable, cornerless shape (it prefigures the actual ring leitmotif from the *Ring* cycle), perfectly suited to infest Elsa's mind.

The scene of recrimination and then renewed alliance between Ortrud and Telramund has a penetrating psychological
momentum that is the operatic equivalent to the tauntings of
Lady Macbeth. The sudden, indescribably moving shift in temperature during the transition to Elsa's appearance proves how
assuredly Wagner has learned to allow the music to speak in
the joints during which the libretto is silent. This is even more
evident during the torturous pauses in the final scene before
the minster as Elsa attempts to quash her doubts.

It's a good thing that most wedding planners remain blissfully unaware of Wagner's irony in setting up the idyllic,
ultrafamous bridal music at the top of act 3. Its stately dotted
rhythms are a counterpart to the trumpet fanfares that sadly
announce the dawn after Elsa has asked the forbidden question and thereby unwittingly destroyed the marriage in its first
hours. This enframing, worldly music suggests a ritualistic quality that has captured the imagination of directors such as Robert
Wilson, whose famous 1998 production of *Lohengrin* required
the actors to step in an exaggerated slow motion while freeze-
framing to hieratic gestures. In between the wedding and the
dawn, however, Wagner allows Lohengrin and Elsa to blend
in a unified, breathlessly lovely new stretch of lyrical pathos.
Underneath, one can hear echoes of the earlier Romantics and
of Italianate melody. As was discussed earlier, the bel canto
style had made a deep impression on the young Wagner; it was
a style that he never ceased to love, however far he departed
from its aesthetic.

In *Lohengrin,* the flow between scenes and subsections is
more successfully integrated than in *Tannhäuser.* And Wagner's
recurrent use of themes evoking the Grail, Elsa, Ortrud, and
the forbidden question prefigures the leitmotif in a basic sense.
Wagner hardly invented the concept of the leitmotif (also
spelled "leitmotiv"), that is, of a recurring musical theme that

becomes associated with an aspect of a character or even an idea (he didn't in fact use the term, but instead referred to a "Grundthema," or "basic theme"). But its elaboration into a tool of ingenious psychological complexity has become by far the best-known example of Wagnerian innovation, often referenced by people who have never encountered a single Wagner opera in its entirety. *Lohengrin* clearly hints at a rudimentary leitmotif technique, but it's easy to exaggerate the significance of Wagner's more mechanical use of such reference points here before the epoch-making musico-dramatic advances ushered in by the *Ring* cycle. At the same time, *Lohengrin* represents the culmination of the grand romantic opera genre that Wagner had once set out to conquer. It contains the magnificent choral writing and ensemble pieces, duets, and arias that one expects from this tradition. But even within those expectations, Wagner infuses something new.

A prime example is Lohengrin's "Grail Narration" after Elsa has posed the forbidden question, "In fernem Land" ("In a far distant land") (CD 1, track 4). At first hearing, this is another aria. Yet instead of stopping the action merely to flesh out the character's feelings or state of mind, as in a conventional aria, this moment is superbly integrated into its dramatic and musical position. Lohengrin's narration of his origins is after all the tragic climax that he (and the audience) had hoped would be avoided. It is thus a heightened moment for which anticipation had been built up (like a big aria) but is also anticlimactic, an appendage to the tragic exchange that has just occurred between Elsa and Lohengrin. In other words, his narration has proved inevitable as the result of the opera's inherent conflicts. This turns out to be a good strategy to loop us in from a musical point of view. But for all the anticipation that the music creates, it establishes a mood we enter reluctantly, for we know the dramatic significance it spells. Anticipation and dread become intertwined, opposite sides of the same coin. The narration is enveloped in musical material now familiar to the audience (0:01), who have encountered it already in the prelude and in Elsa's dream of longing in act 1. The revelation of Lohengrin's name (4:39) completes the audience's knowledge around this music and repeats the climax of the prelude; yet that very process is what dooms the knight to retreat to his own lonely isolation (3:50). The completion he had hoped to find in Elsa is unattainable, and so Lohengrin is, with a cruel irony, brought full circle to the music with which the opera had begun.

Lohengrin has long been recognized as a figure for Wagner himself as artist. Carl Dahlhaus describes the opera as "the tragedy of the absolute artist." Wagner's previous self-por-traits—as the Dutchman and Tannhäuser—had found, albeit at great cost, a human contact that would prove faithful as a reward for their pioneering journeys. But in *Lohengrin,* the artist is cut off and appears only as a rare miracle in a skeptical society. His contact here only results in his further isolation. The final liberation of Elsa's brother Gottfried, as Ortrud's spell is broken and he is transformed from Lohengrin's swan, almost seems like a distraction. It hardly serves as substitute for the catharsis that never happens, the redeeming act of love that is only transient in the world of *Lohengrin.* Wagner spent considerable time fretting over his choice here, fearing Elsa's punishment would appear too cruel. Yet in the end he decided it was necessary, since "right from the outset...the idea of separa-tion struck me as being [the legend's] most characteristic and uniquely distinguishing feature."

There's a reductionist tendency to view Wagner's art as growing progressively pessimistic through the composition of the *Ring,* in contrast to his presumably earlier, revolutionary optimism. While this view does have a certain validity, the deeply rooted pessimism of *Lohengrin* shows the chronology to be rather more complex. This work, often seen as the epitome of Romantic opera, encodes a highly anti-Romantic message. Like Lohengrin's reluctant song of farewell to his swan, Wagner here bids a bittersweet adieu to the art as he knows it. He will have to find a radically different way to explore his hope that art can make a difference. Saying goodbye to the secure life he has known in Dresden will give him the jolt to embark on that all-consuming project.

5 The World's Breath

Tristan und Isolde

eople who categorically hate Wagner tend to have a weak spot for *Tristan und Isolde*. It might be only grudging respect, but even the most extreme anti-Wagnerian would find it hard to justify an attitude of outright dismissal. Shoring up this status are credentials external to the work itself. Survey courses in the history of Western music have long since enshrined *Tristan* as a seminal cultural moment in the birth of modernism. Wagner's compulsion to stretch his musical language to its limits here forced centuries of traditional tonality to the snapping point. As a result, according to the standard narrative of musical progress, it unlocked a Pandora's box that eventually prepared the way for twentieth-century atonality. And the debt of those subsequent pioneers hardly went unacknowledged. Both Arnold Schoenberg's *Verklärte Nacht* (Transfigured Night) and Alban Berg's *Lyric Suite* pay homage by quoting *Tristan*'s famous opening phrase. Yet even those with little interest in music history are likely to encounter the pervasive *Tristan* in other contexts.

An eloquent witness to the work's potency is the philosopher Friedrich Nietzsche. He once remarked that he could not have imagined surviving adolescence without *Tristan*. Nietzsche's intense reaction inspired his early philosophical manifesto from 1871, *The Birth of Tragedy from the Spirit of*

Music. Its famous dichotomy of the Apollonian (rational) and the Dionysian (instinctive) offered nothing less than a paradigm shift. Although he would later become Wagner's harshest critic and bitterly recant his position, Nietzsche concluded *The Birth of Tragedy* with a panegyric to Wagner's *Tristan* as a work resuscitating the long-forgotten secrets of art revealed by ancient Greece.

Fittingly enough, it was a newfound philosophical enthusiasm that first drove Wagner himself to the tragic love story of Tristan and Isolde. He began to consider it as a suitable topic for his developing art as he was immersed in composition of the *Ring* cycle. A letter to his friend Franz Liszt, dated December 16, 1854, announces Wagner's sudden involvement with the pessimistic philosophy of Arthur Schopenhauer, who "has entered my lonely life like a gift from heaven." His reading of the philosopher's magnum opus, *Die Welt als Wille und Vorstellung* (The World as Will and Representation), provided a shattering epiphany that reverberated through the rest of his life. Wagner regarded his reaction less as a discovery than as a clarification of an outlook to which he had long been predisposed—justifiably so, since one can indeed find traces of this philosophy in his earlier work. Yet the shock of recognition he experienced would have a far more profound effect on his artistic outlook than did his dalliance with the revolutionary political ideas that had brought about Wagner's exile.

Schopenhauer followed the path forged by Kant in exploring the relation between the phenomenal world—the deceptive world of appearances—and its underlying reality. He took a radical turn, however, from both Kant and such idealists as Hegel in finding the nature of ultimate reality to be based on the agency of an irrational, blind, purposeless life-force he called the Will (its Freudian analog would be the id). This Will replicates itself in each human individual and dictates our lives, giving rise to the daily world of appearances, cause and effect, and motivations that we believe we can manipulate. But to follow the Will, which is simply to obey normal human nature, only condemns us to an endless cycle of frustration and unhappiness, for it can never be appeased in this universe, this world without design. Any act to ensure happiness by pursuing our desires is bound to be Sisyphean; we get sucked only deeper into the Will's ever-changing flux. There's really no way out save to pull away the "veil of illusion" distracting us from the reality of this horrific, fundamental Will, and to recognize the suffering that permeates all life. The only hope for redemption is then to renounce the will to live.

That, in crude simplification, is the overall picture that so gripped Wagner. But another key attraction for him was the particular role Schopenhauer assigns to music. In his assessment of human cultural activity, Schopenhauer tends to denigrate the natural sciences as sophisticated distractions to keep us wrapped up in our illusory existence with false notions of "progress"—a useless relic of the Enlightenment. Art, by contrast, provides not a means to a futile end but a state of contemplation that brings us closer to understanding ultimate reality as it is. And music alone has direct access to that reality, just as music alone can convey its essence to the human mind. One can readily imagine how compelling all of this must have appeared to someone of Wagner's temperament, with his own urgent need to account for the world's suffering and to find salvation from perpetual unhappiness. So much so that Wagner almost would have had to invent Schopenhauer if he did not already exist.

The composer's first intensive immersion in this philosophy coincided with his work on *Die Walküre* and would come to shape his subsequent approach to the *Ring* as a whole. Yet Wagner already intuited that another outlet was needed. It's no coincidence that his letter to Liszt extolling the brilliance of Schopenhauer concludes with his first known mention of another myth to tackle, the age-old tale of Tristan and Isolde:

> But since I have never in my life enjoyed the true happiness of love, I intend to erect a further monument to this most beautiful of dreams, a monument in which this love will be properly sated from beginning to end: I have planned in my head a *Tristan* and *Isolde,* the simplest, but most full-blooded musical composition; with the "black flag" which flutters at the end, I shall then cover myself over in order—to die.

This archetypal story of love and passion experienced to the brink provided a vehicle through which he could work out his new preoccupations. Wagner, however, was hardly ready to renounce the Will just yet, particularly when it came to matters of sexual attraction. At the time, the exiled composer had found temporary refuge in Zurich. He relied on a varying string of supporters who kept him from being buried by his chronically catastrophic debts. The pattern became a sort of template: Wagner would win over an ally to his artistic cause, usually as a patron. A circle of admirers formed around him, including very often said ally's spouse. When Wagnerian magnetism captivated the latter's affection, it would precipitate a crisis. Astonishingly, such developments didn't necessarily spell the end of the patron's support—even when Wagner fled and left others to pick up the pieces.

Early in the 1850s the composer had met Otto Wesendonck, a wealthy silk merchant involved in the American market. Wesendonck soon began to offer his extraordinarily generous financial support to Wagner, lasting through most of the decade. Emotional support was likely not foreseen as part of the arrangement. But Wagner inevitably found such in Otto's twenty-three-year-old wife Mathilde; she became the linch-pin of Wagner's relationship with the Wesendoncks. The latter made a cottage on the grounds of their villa outside Zurich available for Wagner and his wife Minna to occupy. Nicknamed the "Asyl" (refuge), this new residence provided an inspiring view of the Alps as well as close proximity to the young, artis-tically inclined Mathilde. She became a powerful muse, and Wagner even set to music five of her poems (the so-called *Wesendonck Lieder*)—a rare case of his composing music to words not written by himself.

In 1857, Wagner returned to the topic of *Tristan* with renewed fervor. He characterized his need to do so as a kind of inner compulsion. The pull made itself felt even as Wagner was immersed in the middle of the *Ring* cycle; it proved powerful enough to cause him to interrupt years of focus on the latter at the end of the second act of *Siegfried*. Aside from some work on orchestration, Wagner would not resume composition of the *Ring* at full speed until 1869. The widespread explanation is that he had become consumed with a passionate love for Mathilde, and its intensity begged for immediate expression in his *Tristan*. Yet one should never lose sight of Wagner's propensity to act out his life as if it were one endless piece of theater. It's perhaps more plausible that the reverse occurred: the composer's need to find a new artistic outlet and to write *Tristan* led him to fall in love as a way to fuel his inspiration. Like the love potion in his music drama, Wagner's creative needs provided the catalyst.

This is one reason that, contrary to what is generally assumed, his affair with Mathilde may actually have been pla-tonic. The key, after all, to the myth of Tristan and Isolde is that their love can never find completion within this existence. So observes Denis De Rougemont in his classic study *Love in the Western World* (first published in 1940). He dissects the earli-est versions of the myth to draw attention to the obstacles to fulfillment embodied in the story: not as enhancements of the plot but as integral to its inner meaning, by which love and death become equated. De Rougemont treats this myth as pivotal to understanding how the idea itself of passionate love developed in the West, describing its origin during a period rife with heresies against establishment Christianity. He decodes the Tristan story as encapsulating pagan and heretical ideas that were forced to go "underground."

These were then circulated widely in disguised and usually unrecognized form through legends and poetry (not unlike the process popularized in Dan Brown's bestselling novel *The Da Vinci Code*). In essence, the hidden meaning of Tristan for De Rougemont involves a Manichean view of a universe: that is, a universe starkly divided between evil (created matter and the physical world) and good (the spirit). Since the power of love is necessarily allied with the good, it yearns for release from the bounds of earthly existence and strives to achieve union in the realm of the spirit rather than communion in this life. In De Rougemont's intriguing hypothesis, Wagner unconsciously taps into this arcane, long-lost core of the myth through the tormented desire given shape by his music.

Whatever form his own love affair with Mathilde took, obstacles most certainly abounded. Wagner buried himself in his new *Tristan* music in the "Asyl," fed by a literary diet of Goethe and the Spanish tragedian Calderon and in frequent conversation with Mathilde. In the spring of 1858 his long-suffering wife Minna intercepted a letter tenderly addressed to Mathilde, wrapped, appropriately, inside a pencil sketch of the epoch-making prelude. This epistolary contact (known as the "morning confession" and mostly filled with ruminations on Goethe's *Faust*) was the final straw for Minna. The idyll in Zurich was broken up and Wagner was forced to flee yet again. Although he was cut off for a time from Mathilde—

her absence doubtless a stimulus to his inspiration—Wagner surprisingly managed to maintain his friendship both with her and with Otto until the end of his life. He returned to the role of wanderer for the next few years, residing variously in France, Italy, and Switzerland. Having varied his standard composition method for *Tristan* (*Siegfried* is the only other work in which he followed the same pattern), he sketched out, drafted, and then completely orchestrated each act before moving on to the next. As a result, Wagner composed the three acts of *Tristan* in separate locations: Zurich, Venice, and Lucerne for acts 1, 2, and 3, respectively. And each exhibits a noticeably distinctive stylistic character, although not at the expense of the remarkable unity of the whole—which Wagner completed in August 1859.

This is the briefest overview of the chief contexts associated with *Tristan:* the watershed in music history it represents, the discovery of Schopenhauer, the biographical obsession with love and its meaning. Yet it barely scratches the surface surrounding a work freighted with such an unusual burden of significance. How amusing then to consider another reason behind Wagner's decision to plunge into *Tristan:* he was convinced he had a moneymaker on his hands. After years of toiling on the *Ring* cycle, Wagner admitted the harsh reality that it might never be staged. *Tristan* by contrast initially seemed as if it might prove to be a highly "practicable" work with a small cast that could start generating the revenue so desperately needed by a man drowning in debt. Wagner whipped up interest from his publishers, and they began engraving the score as he finished each act. When he got wind of the Emperor of Brazil's enthusiasm for his music, he even toyed with the notion of fleeing to South America and preparing a translated version to be given in Rio de Janeiro.

As it turned out, *Tristan* had to wait several years before it was finally ventured on stage. It was, incidentally, the first new work the public had from Wagner since *Lohengrin*—it's hard to imagine how shocking the contrast must have seemed. An attempt to mount *Tristan* in Vienna fell apart after fifty-two rehearsals, when it was declared "unperformable." Finally the premiere was given in June 1865 in Munich, under the direction of one of the greatest of Wagner's interpreters, the maverick conductor Hans von Bülow. This victory, however, was tainted by an ironic echo of the *Tristan* story far more brutal than the situation with the Wesendoncks (who at least remained together as a couple, intact in the Wagnerian wake)—and one ruthlessly caricatured in the press as the *Jerry Springer* episode of its day. Wagner had fallen deeply in love with von Bülow's young wife Cosima, who happened to be a daughter of Franz Liszt. The two would form a partnership as indestructible as that of John and Yoko.

And this time there was no ambiguity about the affair's consummation: just a few months before the premiere, the couple had an illegitimate daughter they named (what else?) Isolde (she later lost her claim to the Wagner legacy). To top it off, a favorite performer of Wagner's, the obese *heldentenor* (heroic tenor) Ludwig Schnorr von Carolsfeld, introduced the demanding role of Tristan only to die of a sudden fever weeks later at the age of twenty-nine. Ever since, a subdued version of the curse lore that surrounds *Macbeth* has been occasionally associated with *Tristan und Isolde*. It certainly remains exceedingly difficult to cast, on account of what it requires of its two lead characters.

Wagner's approach to his *Tristan* source material is consistent with what we have seen in his treatment of myths elsewhere: his attraction is to the universal meaning latent within. He refashions earlier sources, so he believes, to highlight what had become obscured. The retooling provides an extraordinary window into both Wagner's century and his personal obsessions. But unlike his frequent conflation of varied sources elsewhere into a new whole (most notably in the *Ring*), Wagner's process in *Tristan* is above all to strip away. The tendency toward radical expansion that had set the *Ring* in motion—rather like an artistic big bang—now goes in a reverse direction. From a dramatic point of view, compression is of the essence in *Tristan*.

Wagner pursued this process very consciously. Once again, he disparaged his medieval forbear: the thirteenth-century poet Gottfried von Strassburg, whose chivalric romance wove together many elements from the innumerable previous variants of this tale (most likely Celtic in origin). The Tristan and Isolde of legend endure a number of separations over years and deceive King Marke more blatantly (as the tale progresses, two Isoldes in fact are introduced: Queen Isolde and Isolde the Fair). Wagner considered the manifold incidents of Gottfried's narrative to be distracting vagaries, although his libretto does closely echo a number of Gottfried's poetic conceits. In a way that almost anticipates De Rougemont's strategy of decoding the myth (but with a far different intention), Wagner's method is to peer through the specifics of the narrative to discern the paradigm of an extreme, utterly transforming love at its heart.

But he goes even further. Wagner strips down to the essentials of the myth. He keeps external plot to an abstract minimum. This structure then allows him to sustain focus on what he calls the "soul states" of Tristan and Isolde. Wagner's aim is to illuminate his characters from within. As love progresses through them, their soul states, not the events that happen to them, in fact become the real action of the music drama. Wagner drew attention to this quality of *Tristan*: "Life and death, the whole import and existence of the outer world, here hang on nothing but the inner movements of the soul."

All of this opens up an extraordinary new horizon for Wagner's music. The prelude (CD 1, track 5) gives the audience ready access to this inner world in a highly distilled form.

Its very intensity is meant not simply to establish mood but to acclimatize the audience to that inward-directed perspective— rather as the characters in Thomas Mann's *The Magic Mountain* undergo a period of acclimatization to the mountain air surrounding their sanatorium. (Mann in fact wrote an early study for his classic novel in the form of a short story called *Tristan*.) The prelude reminds us of Schopenhauer's idea that music alone can penetrate the false world of appearances, revealing the ultimate reality of the Will. Throughout *Tristan,* the role assigned to music hews closely to this idea. And of course in this music drama, the primary guise of the Will is desire.

The prelude's opening statement, a kind of call (0:01) and response (0:12), has become the emblem for *Tristan*'s music of desire. The two phrases collide in one of music history's most famous chords (0:12). This, the so-called "*Tristan* chord," has generated countless analyses (it is technically a half-diminished seventh, although the usual music theory nomenclature is not really applicable here, since its definitions always depend on harmonic context). It is the same ambiguous chord into which the music resolves at the climax of the prelude (8:16), and it plays a pivotal role throughout the music drama. Another— more conventional—resolution prefigures the ecstatic culmination of the pair's love music (2:04). Still, it's a bit curious that the unique *Tristan* style is routinely described as a harmonic phenomenon. Rapid and daring fluctuations of unusual harmonies indeed permeate the score's vocabulary, but Wagner draws on a wide range of elements beyond harmony for this music of desire.

The prelude's unnerving pauses (they recur in the "Potion" scene of act 1) keep us hanging (e.g., 0:24 or 0:53), while its harmonies are carefully voiced through delicate instrumental combinations (for example, the woody tones of lower winds [10:45]). Most significantly, the linear motion of this opening phrase—after a yearning span, it shifts downward (0:10), then upward (0:17)—announces the kind of music Wagner labeled *infinite melody.* Its obsessive chromaticism and repeated sequences seem to stretch the line endlessly (e.g., 2:32 ff). In composing such music, Wagner noted, his chief problem was one of restraint, "since exhaustion of the theme is quite impos-sible." In collaboration, all these elements effect an unrelenting interplay between tension and release, delay and excitement: the very mechanism Freud later singled out as critical to the libido's workings.

The prelude focuses on a long, dotted-rhythm theme first heard in the cellos (associated with the love glance Isolde exchanges with Tristan) (2:08). It develops other themes as well, but these are so closely interconnected with the first that the whole impression is monothematic, like the *Lohengrin* prelude. Both preludes also trace parallel patterns of gradual crescendo to a large climax (starting at 7:32) followed by a much shorter tapering down—here, to a bare theme in the basses (10:51). But where *Lohengrin* presents a shimmering, lonely sense of harmony, *Tristan's* prelude progressively ratchets up the tension to give voice to desire, naked and disclosed. The brief respites as it wends toward an inevitable climax are like small fires put out and then lit anew (e.g., 4:06 or 4:20). The monothemati-cism here has a new purpose as well: Wagner avoids traditional contrasts of musical material (so evident, for example, in the overture to *Der fliegende Holländer*) to keep our focus on this music of desire as the fundamental element of the drama.

Throughout *Tristan's* score, and in keeping with his depiction of the main characters' soul states, Wagner tends to sustain particular musical atmospheres more completely and to shift between them more subtly. The polarities that are essential to his musico-dramatic imagination are still present, but here they take on a more sophisticated and complex form. Instead of presenting different sound worlds to distinguish groups of characters, Wagner's music is now able to distinguish levels of *consciousness* within his two main characters. One might even trace a broad arc of such shifts in consciousness throughout the entire music drama (reinforced by each act's markedly distinctive musical style). In act 1, focus is on the attempt to deflect desire and the buildup to its unexpected but overwhelming invasion (symbolized by the drinking of the potion). The couple's temporary fusion in act 2 into an ecstasy oblivious to the world around them is prefigured in Isolde's hallucinatory misreadings of the sounds around her in the first scene. In act 3, Wagner takes us to an even further extreme of consciousness (possibly only Beethoven, in his late quartets, had essayed such a depiction), in the delirium of Tristan's separation from Isolde.

Just as the music does, the libretto also makes *Tristan* stand apart. Even if he did publish them as "poems" in their own right, there's always a danger in considering Wagner's texts as separate entities. They simply cannot be unraveled from their total context in the music drama. But it is important to note how Wagner's frequent use of short lines filled with paradox, reversal, and heightened parallelism becomes a kind of mirror for the music's thematic interplay.

The libretto, moreover, continually revolves around these polarities: day and night, illusion and truth, betrayal and loyalty, deception and honesty, love and death. They are blended and reversed in constant paradoxes: day is the source of illusion, night is true; betrayal is committed by the truest of friends; death is the path to lasting life. Even the conjunction *and* of the title is deconstructed in the garden of love as a false barrier. These gain clarity if we again recall Schopenhauer's distinction between the false world of appearances (including the knightly customs in Tristan's world) and the unavoidable truth of the Will. But this is by no means the only perspective informing

Tristan. The famous glorification of night over day, for example, has a very long lineage that is also woven into Wagner's
music drama: the dark night of the soul of the Christian mys-
tics, as well as the extraordinarily beautiful *Hymnen an die
Nacht* (Hymns to the Night) of the great early Romantic poet
Novalis.

The leitmotifs in *Tristan* are more ambiguous than in the
early parts of the *Ring*. They are even more difficult to name
(usually a mistaken impulse, in any case, whether the issue is
the *Ring* or other mature works). They interrelate in richly
woven, symphonic patterns that further emphasize their constantly shifting associative functions. Take act 1, which first
portrays Isolde at length, smoldering with humiliation and a
thirst for revenge. She hopes to effect this through the death
potion she plans for Tristan. Her emotions are of course reflections of the Will—and variants at that of a deeper, fundamental
desire for Tristan, which is exactly what the music tells us.
Similarly, Tristan's entrance before Isolde is accompanied by a
stiff, ritualistic sort of fanfare. It perfectly corresponds to the
haughty pride and status of Tristan before the two unmask their
desire via the love potion. This is the very theme that will be
transformed into the couple's ecstatic love music.

That famous love music at the core of act 2 (to call it a
duet is an understatement, for it's beyond category) takes us
deep within the characters now that they have begun their
transformation by love. Wagner finds an amazing variety of
expressive ways to depict their soul states: from erotic impetuosity to silky, veiled melodies that float upward and, finally, to
ecstatic otherworldliness. All this he renders with a palettelike
approach to orchestration—and one scarcely notices how he
allows the lovers' voices actually to blend only at the climax.
The one thing one is spared is cheap sentimentality. Wagner's
love music in *Tristan* was a source of scandal in his day and is

intimately connected with his reputation as a "sensualist" com-poser. Commentators have even gone so far in their biological interpretation of the score as to identify exact moments of orgasm and detumescence (a tactic that is quite easy to do in the prelude to Richard Strauss's *Der Rosenkavalier*, where it is comic, and in Shostakovich's *Lady Macbeth of Mtsensk*, where it is darkly sardonic). Yet it's crucial to keep in mind the larger context, however easy it is to be pulled into the world of the lovers. For it's the larger perspective, *beyond* Tristan and Isolde, that really concerns Wagner in this music drama.

Brangäne's role is brilliantly realized in this regard. She is the sentinel who stands guard at the liminal zone between night and day (the devoted servant Kurwenal serves a very parallel function for Tristan in act 3). She lingers between the normal world and the heightened one of the lovers, bridging its shift in consciousness but not partaking of it. But Brangäne is also the one to see that the lovers' capitulation to desire cannot bring a happiness that lasts. Her melancholy, Cassandra-like cry of warning contains some of the most beautiful music in *Tristan*, for it expresses a reluctant acceptance of this truth.

King Marke's lengthy monologue at the end of the act, after the lovers have been interrupted, similarly brings back a realis-tic perspective. This is actually a masterstroke (counterintuitive as it is). Marke is presented not as an unwanted intruder but as a sympathetic figure who desperately wants to understand his betrayal. (The brief role of Melot, who plotted the discovery of the lovers, is the only one that comes close to traditional melodrama.) Tristan's response that he *cannot* explain—for Marke has not yet seen through the veil of illusion and there-fore cannot possibly understand—is a deeply moving key to his experience of love. It will reach its climax in the final act. The problem is that this scene is quite difficult to bring off in performance from the point of view of staging. The director's nightmare is to decide what to do with the suddenly mute Isolde (Birgit Nilsson's unbeatable quip was to wear "a comfortable pair of shoes").

Act 3 brings home the larger vision of *Tristan.* The music of intense suffering that permeates Tristan's monologues elevates the drama to a new level. It now becomes clearer that Wagner's "monument to this most beautiful of dreams" is not just a steamy love story, if one is still tempted to mistake it as such. Many listeners tend to assume that *Tristan und Isolde* is the apo-theosis of romantic passion. Wagner's success in depicting the emotions and primal urges of desire is stunning, and arguably unsurpassed. Yet this is only part of the story, part of the music drama. Rather than a glorification of passion, *Tristan* is to a large degree about overcoming it. The hero's interior journey in act 3 is harrowing and partakes more than ever in the mystic's dark night of the soul. Wagner is highly calculating in how he allows the music to weave in and out of Tristan's consciousness, back to the reactions of the external world (represented by Kurwenal and the shepherd, who alternate between melancholy and eager hope). As the music heats up to fever pitch in his staggered states of delirium, its excitement evokes nothing of the erotic character heard earlier in the drama. Its depiction of an empti-ness at the core of desire is nothing short of terrifying, and this very realization fuels Tristan's suffering. This is what the word *passion* after all signifies in its root meaning.

During the years of his involvement with *Tristan,* Wagner had begun reading books about Buddhism. His fascination would have been reinforced by Schopenhauer's own acknowledgment of a debt to that religion in formulating his philosophy. Indeed, Wagner had even contemplated composing a music drama called *Die Sieger* (The Victors) based on a Buddhist parable. Some of those impulses may well have been deflected into this final act of his *Tristan.* There's a recognizably Buddhist undertone in the imagery of light being quenched and breath dying away. A touching moment—one of the opera's most indelible—occurs in Tristan's panic over seeing Isolde still in the clutch of light and the day. It marks a transformation. Tristan has evolved from his erotic idea of love to a capacity for disinterested, spiritual love. Like a bodhisattva—a saint who returns to lead the still unenlightened to peace—Tristan's compassion compels him to return from his state of enlightenment and seek out Isolde, who has remained behind.

The story's logic, as we have seen, dictates that the lovers cannot be united in this world. But in Isolde's final scene, she too undergoes a remarkable transformation that far more serenely recapitulates what Tristan achieved in his tortured visions. Wagner subtly shifts the focus away from the turmoil surrounding her, with its *Hamlet*-like accumulation of corpses. In a flash of genius, from the starting moments (CD 1, track 6), he reverts to the love music heard at the height of act 2 but carefully modulates it into a slower, less hectic lyricism. The effect is instead oceanic and corresponds to what Isolde tries to express. In place of the erotic tension and heated tempo of the second act's love music, Isolde ascends to a high A-flat on the word "shines" (0:43), literally above the situations she's experiencing in the real world. She seeks to merge "in the heaving swell/in the ringing sound/in the boundless wave/of the world's breath" (4:34 ff). The music's ecstatic climax is often characterized as a musical orgasm (4:47 ff) and is here given its complete expression, in contrast with its prior (interrupted) appearance in the act 2 duet. The gorgeously prepared, perfectly spaced final B major chord, which resolves the drama as well as the harmonic ambiguity evoked at the very beginning of the prelude, ends with a crescendo and then dies out, like one final primal breath (6:34 to end).

This is the so-called *Liebestod* (love-death), although Wagner actually gave that label to the prelude (as if to indicate the music where desire is still in command) and called Isolde's song a "transfiguration." The effect of a breakthrough here is indescribable. In a sense, this depiction of Isolde's nirvana, where she has found release from the compulsion of blind Will, becomes a metaphor for what Wagner has discovered his art can do. Certainly that was the experience of Nietzsche when he declared, in *The Birth of Tragedy,* that "only as an aesthetic phenomenon are existence and the world eternally justified."

A Touch of Madness

The Creative Spirit and
Die Meistersinger von Nürnberg

The contrasts between *Tristan und Isolde* and *Die Meistersinger von Nürnberg* (The Mastersingers of Nuremberg) must rank among the starkest in the career of any artist. Like the man himself, Wagner's music dramas abound with polarities and internal contradictions. They play a deeply needed role in stimulating his imagination. But nowhere are the polarities *between* works created in sequence so strikingly conspicuous. Someone first encountering the shift in basic demeanor from *Tristan* to *Die Meistersinger*, both in emotional atmosphere and in musical expression, might be tempted to assume a multiple personality disorder in their creator.

Die Meistersinger is the sole "official" comedy from the Wagner canon. He did pursue the genre elsewhere in his early thinking around *Siegfried*, and savvy directors know that the image of Wagner as unchangeably serious and dusk-obsessed ignores the presence of comic undertones in a number of scenes. But Wagner's only other complete comedy is his rarely seen, youthful version of Shakespeare, the opera *Das Liebesverbot*. In *Die Meistersinger*, for once we are spared separation and/or death as the drama's inevitable conclusion; instead, we witness a triumph of love in the classic sense. As for his characters, Wagner cannot resist introducing his archetypal outsider in the figure of the artist Walther, but in a softened version. *Die Meistersinger* notably lacks the extremity of desperate alienation, of being pushed to the limits of existence, so crucial elsewhere in Wagner. Parody and satire seem to take the place of fate, while in contrast to the profoundly antisocial perspective of *Tristan*, the social community plays a central role in *Die Meistersinger.* In the latter, *Tristan*'s pared-down simplicity of dramatic struc-ture gives way to a storyline full of detailed interchanges and subplots. A specific historical setting replaces timeless, mythic soul states. It's as if Wagner here renounces the dark night of *Tristan* in favor of life-affirming multiplicity: a denial of denial. Magnifying all these contrasts is a musical language of assertively diatonic energy. It provides a framework for internal harmonic ambiguities, rather than a counterpart to them. The resulting sound world, superficially at least, seems planets apart from *Tristan*'s chromatic languor and indeterminacy.

And yet both are unmistakably Wagnerian. Their coexis-tence is a powerful example of Wagner's ability to create worlds complete and distinct from one another from one music drama to the next. There is, to be sure, a common thread of obses-sively repeated themes that runs through them (Wagner even imagined characters from one opera wandering into another, as if the operas were interconnected rooms of a mansion). Yet each exists apart, evolving its unique language and atmosphere. Think of the different spheres inhabited by each Beethoven symphony or by *Hamlet* in contrast to *King Lear.* Yet the mag-netic presence *behind* these unique works binds them together through a sense of fundamental unity. Even after experiencing the soul-searching breakthrough inspired by his discovery of Schopenhauer, Wagner was able to reconcile his earlier achieve-ments (including ongoing work on the *Ring*) with his new out-look. Similarly, as will be seen, there are threads connecting *Die Meistersinger* with *Tristan*—despite all their marked antith-eses. The two operate on a deeper level as a complementary whole. Not unlike the relation of Eugene O'Neill's (equally rare) comedy *Ah, Wilderness!* to *Long Day's Journey into Night*, *Die Meistersinger* and *Tristan* display two sides of the same coin.

But we are, after all, dealing with Wagner: the notion of comedy is not as straightforward as it might seem at first glance. Like the *Ring* and *Parsifal*, *Die Meistersinger* underwent a lengthy period of maturation between its genesis and the scoring over two decades later of the blazing C major with which the opera concludes. Wagner first conceived the idea behind *Die Meistersinger* during that fertile summer of 1845 spent taking the waters at the Marienbad spa (which had also yielded the plan for *Lohengrin*, along with other projects). In the aftermath of the recently premiered *Tannhäuser*, with its focal singing contest, his reading in the history of German literature had suggested another opera based on a similar singing competition—but in a more cheerful vein. Wagner imagined something along the lines of the lighthearted, comic satyr plays that followed the tragic trilogies presented during theater festivals in ancient Greece. In July he drafted his first prose scenario for *Die Meistersinger*. (What eventually became *Siegfried* shared a parallel plan in its original version as *Der junge Siegfried* [Young Siegfried], a comic counterpart to the grand tragedy that became *Götterdämmerung.*)

In his autobiography (written during the time he was working on *Die Meistersinger*), Wagner recalled his initial flash of inspiration in highly visual terms. He enjoyed imagining a sharp contrast between the figure of the working-class hero and poet Hans Sachs and the "Marker" from the Mastersinger Guild, a pedant charged with keeping track of infractions against the rules of the art. The Marker, in a situation that became the finale of act 2, is forced to taste his own medicine when singing a serenade to his beloved in front of the cobbler Sachs. Having been previously mocked by the Marker's nitpicking, Sachs gets his revenge by hammering away at the shoes in his shop to keep track of the Marker's own mistakes.

The comedy was actually meant to have a personally thera-peutic effect as well. Just as the tragic *Lohengrin* was taking shape in his mind, Wagner's doctors were ordering him to be wary of emotional exertion. His new "merry subject" appealed as a distraction to free its author from "preoccupation with *Lohengrin*." This plan, happily, did not interfere with the latter, and Wagner blithely ignored medical advice. Preoccupations of a wholly other order—social revolution, exile, and eventu-ally the *Ring*—followed upon *Lohengrin*. Another sixteen years passed before Wagner returned to the scenario he had writ-ten in 1845. The completion of *Tristan* had been exhausting, but even more enervating were his attempts to have it per-formed—particularly since *Tristan* itself had been intended as a stageworthy, "practicable" outlet, given his frustration over the apparent pipe-dream that the *Ring* had become. Wagner was growing increasingly anxious to bring a new work before the public. So his original conception for *Die Meistersinger* was a modest one. The diverting satyr play now became a subject "exceptionally rich in good-natured drollery," as he described the planned work in a pitch to his publisher in 1861. Wagner was certain he would soon have a hit because of the "thoroughly light and popular" style of the piece.

And yet even here, Wagner simultaneously boasted of "some-thing quite unexpected and singular." This sounds a central, recurring fantasy for the composer vis-à-vis his audience. Its premise was that he could reconcile what appear to be, and more often than not are, mutually exclusive aims: (a) to be valued for persevering in his unique vision, a vision of unprec-edented ambition and originality that avoided the easy formulas of success; and (b) to be loved simultaneously as a genuinely popular and accessible artist, not an aloof elitist. This is the fantasy at the heart of *Die Meistersinger* itself. Both story and music seek to represent the process of artistic validation.

Following a pattern seen elsewhere, the relatively modest original concept eventually ballooned to gigantic proportions. This "light and popular" entertainment brims with a spirit of abundance, of joyful fertility. Leonard Bernstein once declared that Wagner poured out its music in quarts and gallons. Artistic inspiration is one of *Die Meistersinger*'s pivotal topics—and for that matter, a favorite leitmotif in the composer's correspondence and autobiography. Wagner was always keen to portray the workings of his genius as uncontrived and spontaneous. He typically describes his art as a process involving energies that well up from the unconscious, ready to be tapped when the time is right. This is one of the reasons that Wagner exaggerated the degree to which he was self-taught in his own musical education. More significantly, his view of inspiration is closely linked to the world of dreams. Dreams certainly play a prominent role in the music dramas themselves, from Senta and Elsa's presentiments of the arrival of their respective lovers to Tristan's fevered, illusory dreams of Isolde saving him and Wotan's dream of Valhalla. In *Die Meistersinger*, the inspiration for Walther's "Prize Song" (*Morgenlich leuchtend*) comes to him in a dream.

Dreams likewise figure prominently when Wagner discusses his own creative process. Probably the most famous example is his account of a dream that overtook him while visiting the Italian seacoast town of La Spezia in 1853. According to *Mein Leben*, he lay down in his hotel for a nap, in a state of exhaustion. As he drifted off, a sensation of flowing water grew in intensity to the accompaniment an E-flat major triad, which swirled and fragmented as its motion increased, threatening to drown him before he awoke. Thus Wagner broke through the longest musical dry spell of his career. With the floodgates of inspiration opened again, he began to compose his music for the *Ring*. Or so he would have us believe. In fact there is often evidence of a more prosaic jump-start to Wagner's muse. His accounts after the fact always need to be considered with reasonable skepticism, as would be common sense with any artist. Particularly so with Wagner, since the composer's fanciful descriptions of his modus operandi often apply poetic license to the facts. But even considered as a parable, the message Wagner draws from this anecdote is clear: "the vital flood would come from within me, and not from without."

From "within": that doesn't preclude his sympathetic response to preexisting art as an equally valid source of inspiration, a spur to that inner, spontaneous voice. Wagner repeatedly pays homage in his writings to Beethoven as a kind of musical Columbus who opened the way to explore new paths in tone. More concretely, Beethoven's music belongs to the complex amalgam of influences that Wagner melted down and forged into his own voice. *Die Meistersinger* seeks to reconcile both sources—the personal, unmediated dream world of inspiration and the art of past masters that must be built on—as the seed from which genuinely worthwhile art can spring. To borrow T. S. Eliot's celebrated formulation, *Die Meistersinger* is very much about the interweaving of tradition and the individual talent.

Both appear in a curious mix in Wagner's genesis anecdote for *Die Meistersinger.* He writes in his autobiography of meeting up in Venice with the Wesendoncks in November 1861 (their friendship having miraculously survived intact through the *Tristan* crisis). Determined to cheer up a depressed Wagner, the Wesendoncks took him on an art-viewing expedition. The composer's reaction to Titian's *Assumption of the Virgin* proved overpowering. Most likely this is another of Wagner's fanciful spins—he'd already sent his publisher the above-mentioned letter about his decision to plunge back into the *Meistersinger* project—but it does vividly illustrate his desire to draw a connection with the art of the "old masters." Titian's painting serves as an unexpected catalyst though. Wagner showed a frequent indifference to the visual arts. And why, despite the German nationalism that is an essential part of *Die Meistersinger*'s fabric, an Italian master? Could it be that Wagner means to evoke nostalgia for an especially well-known Renaissance utopia in which individual artistic genius was valued as an integral part of society?

As for the source within, Wagner reports of his return from Venice via train to Vienna, where he was living at the time, and suddenly conceiving "the main part" of the complex, intricately woven prelude to *Die Meistersinger* "with the greatest clarity." Yet the work turned out to be unusually effortful and still required a good deal of time to come into being. Wagner returned to his original draft for the libretto from 1845 and fleshed it out in a number of different directions. "Fanget an!" (Begin!) is the recurrent directive in *Die Meistersinger* to a contestant poised to begin his song. But after his own beginning with the prelude, Wagner faced a number of interruptions in his composition and took another five years to finish his draft of the full score.

One can hardly single out any decade from Wagner's tempestuous career as more fraught with drama than the rest. But it is safe to say that the mid-1860s, when he was composing this opera, contained two events of paramount importance that altered his life forever. The first involved falling in love with Cosima von Bülow, the woman who would bring Wagner the greatest degree of emotional stability he was ever to know in his long litany of failed relationships. In her fiercely independent intelligence—and high degree of neurosis, one might add— Wagner found for the first time a mate with whom he could be compatible. Although not conventionally attractive (as a child she was nicknamed "Stork"), Cosima also shared with Wagner a passionately sexual nature.

She was Wagner's junior by a quarter century, an illegitimate daughter of Franz Liszt. She had been married at a young age to the brilliant pianist and conductor and Wagner champion Hans von Bülow. (Bülow's impact on performance history is often underestimated: his rigorous method of rehearsal inspired a desperately needed sense of professionalism in opera companies.) Like Wagner's own unfortunate, now mostly estranged relationship with his first wife Minna, it was not a happy marriage. Wagner had met Cosima several times in the past. By 1864 they had declared mutual love and began living together in a household along with Cosima's two daughters. Minna died in 1866, and when Cosima's marriage was finally dissolved in 1870, she became Wagner's second wife. Bülow meanwhile remained faithful to the Wagnerian cause, a brilliant champion who introduced *Tristan* to the world in 1865, as well as *Die Meistersinger*, in a triumphant premiere on June 21, 1868.

The other life-changing event sounds like the sort of thing Wagner might have dreamed up in his autobiography as a rescue fantasy if it had not actually happened. Although he had been granted amnesty in 1860 for his part in the 1849 Revolution and was at last able to return to German territory, the composer again found himself in dire straits because of his overwhelming burden of debts. He had been forced to flee Vienna in March 1864 to avoid prison. In the same month, an eighteen-year-old monarch ascended the throne as King Ludwig II of Bavaria. Ludwig had been obsessed with Wagner's art since attending a performance of *Lohengrin*. Now in power, he tracked down the incredulous composer to offer whatever financial assistance he needed from Bavaria's state coffers.

The handsome, eccentric, gay young king developed a stormy emotional relationship with the decidedly heterosexual Wagner. To keep the funds flowing, the latter encouraged Ludwig's adoration with endlessly fawning letters, signing off as "loving and true unto death," "faithful in body and soul to my most glorious friend," and the like. For years Ludwig provided generous financial backing that freed Wagner from his persistent financial angst and allowed him to indulge his penchant for luxury. His notorious satins and silks and expensive perfumes, powdered for sprinkling about his chambers, were legitimized as essential ingredients to spur his creativity. ("His tastes in clothing and interior decoration," remarked W. H. Auden, "were those of a drag queen.")

Courtiers hostile to Wagner's influence on the young king eventually chased the composer out of Munich. But the money continued to flow. In 1866 he settled into an idyllic home with Cosima at Triebschen on Lake Lucerne; there he remained situated until choosing his last home in Bayreuth in 1872. Soon after Wagner sequestered himself in Triebschen, the king paid a secret visit. He pretended to be "Walther von Stolzing," the proud knight from *Die Meistersinger,* and announced his desire to abdicate so he could live with the composer. That disaster was averted, although it meant lying to Ludwig about the true nature of Wagner's relationship with Cosima. The king was given the impression that she was an exceptionally gifted secretarial aide.

Such was the backdrop against which Wagner continued work on *Die Meistersinger.* Its creation, from the time he decided to write the opera in 1861, therefore spans a period of extreme contrast in his life, from a state of chaotic insecurity to one of confidence and affirmation. The sunny, "anti-*Tristan*" disposition was there from the start. But the rare moments of personal happiness experienced by the chronically restless composer as he was creating it may have ripened into the exuberant abundance that so characterizes the score. A spirit, too, of reawakened youth illumines the love story of Walther and Eva, as if the middle-aged Wagner found himself able again to tap into long-forgotten moods of promise and possibility.

At the same time, the "thoroughly light" comedy he had projected grew not only in length but in emotional scope. Writing to Mathilde Wesendonck on his birthday (May 22, 1862), when he sketched out ideas for the sublime act 3 prelude, Wagner observed that "this work will be my most perfect masterpiece." The opera's loftier perspective emerges in the portrait of Hans Sachs. As fleshed out, he is a figure of glowing, gently melancholy humanism who dwarves the "jovially poetic" cobbler-poet described in 1861. Sachs has a considerable fan base of opera lovers who consider him none other than Wagner's most fully rounded character, not even excepting Wotan. A parallel from fiction might be how Dickens allowed the episodic, superficial hilarity of his first sketches of Samuel Pickwick for *The Pickwick Papers* to evolve into an archetype of humanity, one of his most admirably genial creations.

Curiously, central as he already was to the story in the original draft, Sachs is absent from the prelude (he receives his own spotlight in the prelude to act 3, a veritable tone poem based on his character). Otherwise, this marvel of orchestral tapestry numbers among Wagner's most excerpted pieces in the concert hall. It also signals a return to the more old-fashioned, overture-style "synopsis" that he had not used since *Tannhäuser*—although Wagner designates it a "Vorspiel" (prelude). But the prelude to *Die Meistersinger* is much more tightly woven, a kind of miniature symphony that encapsulates a précis of the basic story line. In other words, it marries concern with form and structural cohesion to the content that will unfold in the music drama. This process replicates—or rather, foreshadows—precisely what is the central issue at stake in *Die Meistersinger*: the transformation of artistic vision from a fleeting moment of inspired spontaneity into lasting craft that can be shared for posterity. It's a remarkably sophisticated strategy—and a fascinating alternative to the kind of "acclimatization" represented by *Tristan*'s prelude.

Opening in C major, with an attitude both majestic and self-important, the prelude immediately characterizes the proud world of the Mastersingers. Soon a sweetly cadenced, lyrical theme announces a space more private—the love of Walther and Eva—followed by further Meistersinger ideas, more love music of a heightened ardency, and a key tune from the "Prize Song." All of this gives just a hint of the profusion of melodic ideas with which the prelude spills over. This too might seem the antithesis of the monothematic impression exuded by the *Tristan* prelude. Actually, though, one of the signatures of Wagner's art here is to use an extraordinary economy. He pays homage to one of the most enduring of all aesthetic tenets: to create a sense of unity amid the variety. And indeed, much of the entire opera's motivic web is already contained here. Musicologists have gone to town analyzing the interconnections among these ideas. The love theme, for instance, is related to the first part of Walther's "Prize Song," underscoring his triumph in both art and love by the end of the opera. Wagner tailors his "scherzo" by speeding up the Meistersinger's opening march, adding mock-counterpoint, and changing the instrumentation to chattering woodwinds, giving the audience at the same time a snapshot of Beckmesser's annoying personality.

Throughout the opera itself, Wagner continues to fashion leitmotifs around individuals, groups of characters, or events: Walther and his artistic aspiration, Sachs, Beckmesser, the Mastersingers and their guild, *Johannistag* (St. John the Baptist's Day or Midsummer's Day, around which the action is centered), the young lovers, David and the Apprentices, and so on. He distinguishes this diversity of leitmotifs by using keenly identifiable characteristics, sometimes highlighting a melodic interval, a rhythmic pattern, or a harmonic sequence. But these musical "characters," distinct on one level in their dramatic function, are more subtly linked to each other, exactly as the economical spinning of interrelated motives heard in the pre-lude foreshadows.

A crucial difference between *Die Meistersinger* and Wagner's preceding scores is that his musical characterization here relies less on clearly articulated contrasts or polarities between sound worlds. Instead, there's a new compositional focus on the old-fashioned virtue of *polyphony* (literally, "many voices"). What intrigues Wagner is the multiple ways in which these differing musical aspects can be recombined—and brought together simultaneously—into one sound. The interlocking of separate aspects of the opera becomes a kind of sonic metaphor for the central role of community so prominent in *Die Meistersinger*. In a tour de force of counterpoint, the final part of the prelude celebrates this polyphonic idea, underlining how crucial a role it will play in bringing together old and new. The stops are pulled out as all the themes previously introduced, and all they symbolize, get woven together into a joyful, intricate panoply. Walther's visionary inspiration, it turns out, blends euphoni-ously with the once oppressive world of tradition represented by the Mastersingers. We hear the same reconciling C major peroration that will conclude the opera.

Polyphonic textures are indeed blended in high relief at piv-otal moments in the story. These cover an extreme range. The manic counterpoint of the riot finale to act 2 is sheer comic virtuosity, but it also threatens to burst into cacophony just as the crowd nearly disrupts the social order. Only the interrup-tion of the Night Watchman's horn cuts short the dissipation into violence (both social and musical). On the other extreme is the indescribable perfection of the quintet in act 3, "Selig, wie die Sonne" (Blissfully, like the sun). It links the triumph of art and love, but with a subtly shaded, bittersweet refinement accounting for multiple perspectives (including Sachs's gentle renunciation of his claims to Eva's love). Not a bad choice, if you were allowed to preserve only five minutes from all of Wagner in a time capsule. The composer would have appreciated the honor's irony: that a traditional vocal ensemble—fossil of that horror of horrors, grand opera, and declared anathema in his theory for the music of the future—could be a vehicle after all for the most sublime art. This is just one of many instances throughout *Die Meistersinger* in which Wagner bids farewell to the theories announced in *Opera and Drama*—in many ways it marks his own reconciliation with operatic tradition.

One reversal that is impossible to miss plays out in Wagner's young lovers. The pattern of disappointment and separation, of love's impossibility in this world, is by now a familiar Wagnerian theme. Eva introduces a new woman who doesn't need to flee the conditions surrounding her after all (although she and Walther are tempted to elope). As if hints we saw in *Tannhäuser*'s Elisabeth have been fully fleshed out, Eva knows what she wants and is comfortable with her desires. And unlike Isolde, her desires aren't exaggerated to do double duty as a metaphor for humanity's blind will. She's able to contemplate manipulating desire (in acknowledging Sachs's attraction) but is even more susceptible to being swayed by genuine compassion for his loneliness. In short, Eva exhibits a brand of realism that is new for Wagner. She isn't a superwoman whose function is to redeem; her role, which is more down-to-earth—and precisely for that reason, more effective—is to inspire. The Brünnhilde-turned-human at the end of *Siegfried* (and beginning of *Götterdämmerung*) will be seen to share some of this quality. Wagner conveys this shift through a more convention-ally melodic inflection in her music. Significantly, it is Eva who sets the chain of personal epiphanies in motion by beginning the quintet. The orchestral equivalent of her lyricism is the softer, more intimate palette Wagner explores in his orchestration. It deploys notably reduced forces compared to the *Ring* orchestra, with a preponderance of elegant woodwind writing.

Die Meistersinger is the only example from his completed operas in which Wagner invented his narrative more or less wholesale, instead of rearranging, adapting, or paring it down from earlier sources. Rather than turning to mythic material, he drew on research into the medieval guilds and singing contests, musicological artifacts, and of course such historical personalities as the Reformation poet Hans Sachs. Why the sudden commitment to a specific historical situation? And why the apparent reversal of his principles of abstraction in favor of a plot with lots of incidental detail—a counterpart to his musical reversal in allowing for grand chorus, processions, and even a dance, as well as closed forms such as arias and a vocal quintet? As a mere speculation, perhaps this has to do with Wagner's attempt to come to terms with failures from his past, in a kind of repetition complex. *Die Meistersinger* may signal a desire to prove that he could also "do" old-fashioned grand opera better than ever before and on his terms. (The recent debacle of his revised *Tannhäuser*—in 1861 in Paris—must have reawakened his nightmarish memories of the years of youthful dejection in the French capital. It was during this return trip to Paris, after all, that he began writing the *Meistersinger* libretto.)

There is, in addition, a more thematically relevant reason for the historical Nuremberg of the sixteenth century in which *Die Meistersinger* is situated. His years of exile had left Wagner unmoored, exacerbating his recurrent self-identification with the wanderer, the outsider. Fantasies of a utopian community—dedicated, of course to the highest ideals of art, meaning Wagnerian art—are integral to his theoretical musings about the artwork of the future. But with the flood of emotions opened up by his return to German territories in the 1860s, Wagner replaced many of the cherished images of ancient Greece that had formerly played that role with ones from German culture. This was simultaneously the decade in which modern Germany was beginning to modernize. As the growing pains of industrialization took hold and Bismarck maneuvered, Germany was on the verge of uniting (belatedly, like Verdi's Italy) into a single nation-state. This complicated political background of conflicting tendencies—nationalist pride hand in hand with the alienating effects of incipient modernity—colored Wagner's perceptions of old Nuremberg, a cliché of beloved Gothic spires and skyline.

The city of Nuremberg offered a patriotic counterpart to the self-sufficient Greek polis in which art and work were integrated. An American parallel with similar resonance might be some mix of Thornton Wilder's *Our Town* and images of old-time New York City. Along with this nostalgic utopia, Nuremberg represents a microcosm of Reformation human-ism. Sachs, with his research into "world history" mentioned at the beginning of his act 3 monologue (CD 1, track 7), has a touch of Faust, while the presence of Albrecht Dürer and Martin Luther is also felt. Wagner developed a deliberately archaic language for his libretto. He modeled this in part on Luther's German, much like—as will be seen—he revived ancient *Stabreim* (alliterative verse) to give an archaic flavor to his *Ring* poem. The text abounds in *Knittelvers*, the unadorned, irregular short-verse rhyming couplets most famously used by Goethe in *Faust*. More complex rhyme schemes and meters also appear, while Wagner further draws attention to the language of his characters with constant word play. The pun-addicted composer's verbal games have a corollary in the musical trans-formation of themes.

Wagner steeped himself in researching older musical styles and antique modes as he prepared his score. (Interestingly, his presumed nemesis Brahms shared an interest in "early music" and collected old manuscripts. He even expressed admiration for *Die Meistersinger.*) The opera is colored with all sorts of examples of this research. The young apprentice David's strained attempt in act 1 to explain the taxonomy of song types and styles for Walther's benefit is an elaborate in-joke. But it's also a poke at an entire line of thinking about music history (a powerful movement in the heyday of the historicist nineteenth century): the line Ferruccio Busoni so aptly describes represented by "lawgivers" who regard "form as a symbol," thus turning it "into a fetish, a religion."

Wagner's use of this source material is analogous to his manipulation of literary sources in adapting myths into an idiosyncratic personal myth: rather than a pastiche, he constructs a musical language that is very much his own. Even the Bach-like chorales of the community and the archaic-sounding passages of the Mastersingers become absorbed into Wagner's recognizable musical language. A famous instance is the trick he pulls to open the opera itself. The prelude seems to reach a resolute conclusion, assertively hammering out C major power chords: an unequivocal nineteenth-century rhetorical flourish signaling "The End." Yet Wagner makes this ending a beginning through the way in which he segues immediately into the opening scene. The prelude's final chord morphs into resounding organ strains as the congregation intones a Bach-like chorale (he might well have "borrowed" the idea from an opera he greatly admired, Halévy's *La Juive*, which opens with a very similar strategy). The orchestra's multi-voiced peroration meanwhile transforms into the congregation's many voices. The switch from secular to sacred (and very soon back to secular, as the love music of the young pair emerges) suggests the common aims of art and religion in high-Wagnerian fashion.

Carl Dahlhaus observes the self-conscious way in which *Die Meistersinger*'s emphatic diatonicism is built up. His essay in *Richard Wagner's Music Dramas* analyzes how the robust C major of the opening measures subtly, subliminally even, incorporates the destabilizing harmonic tricks of which Wagner was a pioneer. The result conveys a "dreamlike" impression, which is "not so much restoration as reconstruction." "Nowhere," according to Dahlhaus, "is Wagner's music so artificial as in the appearance of simplicity with which it clothes itself in *Die Meistersinger*." And art, including all the artifice that goes into its creation, is the central preoccupation of the opera.

Even the love story is seen through the prism of art. The opening scenes establish that although their mutual love is clear from the start, Walther will have a chance at winning Eva only through conforming in some way to the community's expectations for art. One other option does exist (and is thwarted in act 2): elopement and escape from Nuremberg. But that entails leaving, taking Eva/Eve (Wagner plays repeatedly on the Biblical reference) out of the Paradise or utopia Nuremberg is set up to represent.

Meanwhile, the satirical subplot with Beckmesser also draws on the love-art connection. Wagner no doubt borrows the classically comic archetype of the inappropriately older suitor here. But one of the reasons the audience is *shown* why Beckmesser cannot be a serious candidate for Eva's love is the ridiculous insufficiency of his art (this apart from Sachs's calculated interruptions with his "Cobbler's Song"). Beckmesser's serenade is mechanical and devoid of feeling; no amount of Viagra can mend his appeal.

The links between art and love, Wagner is careful to illustrate, are a two-way road. True love might inspire Walther's art, but true art is needed to win his love. The inspiration is only the beginning of a more involved process. Eva provides the first but is tough enough to encourage the latter through all the opera's trials and errors. Walther first takes the "singer's chair" in his failed audition to be accepted as a Mastersinger with his song "Fanget an!" Its profusion of imagery and rapturous musical setting are almost a self-parody of the emotional overload of, say, *Tristan*. In a sense, the very ardor of his song seems to evoke the Will's power—and however happily the love story turns out, Schopenhauer always looms as a presence following the moment of Wagner's pivotal discovery of the philosopher. Walther's performance makes the case for the merits of direct inspiration; that, however, is not the whole story. It would be too easy to read Walther's rejection as a simple result of the Mastersingers' stodginess and inflexibility. Wagner manipulates the eternal conflict of generations, of old and new, to engage our involvement in what is at stake. But the opera gains in richness by showing that there is a legitimate reason that Walther has yet to emerge as a full-fledged artist.

That process is what Hans Sachs enables. His role as the opera's more complicated hero reminds us how far the work had evolved since Wagner's original satyr play image of a battle between Sachs and the pedantic Marker (Beckmesser). The germinal idea was, after all, a transparent revenge fantasy at the expense of Wagner's critics. In its final form, the composer essentially paints a self-portrait split into two, with all the ensuing contradictions: Wagner is both Walther and Sachs. Each needs the other to complete his (and the audience's) understanding of what art can achieve. Act 1 introduces Sachs as a respected figure, but he's ready to stick his neck out to suggest improvements to the code of musical values the Mastersingers safeguard. It is his idea to make the annual Midsummer's songfest a less elitist event, subject to the vote of the populace.

He also defends the newcomer Walther's awkward position as a singer worth hearing out. Both ideas expose Sachs to ridicule but are validated by the opera's ending.

Wagner could have created a rather tiresome, know-it-all, holier-than-thou figure in Sachs. Instead, he gives the character human depth and kindness. His act 2 monologue "Wie duftet doch der Flieder" (How redolent the elder tree's scent) takes us by surprise and brings us closer to the character's humanity. It illustrates Sachs's own vulnerability as he acknowledges something missing in his world view. He is haunted by the art Walther introduces because it moves him, yet he doesn't understand why and isn't even sure he grasps it. As the teacher becomes student, his admiration for Walther and the epiphany the young man stimulates motivates Sachs to help the lovers, thus setting the rest of the plot in motion.

Wagner pursues this theme of Sachs as enabler in the artistic process most profoundly in act 3. Sachs, as mentioned, was missing from the opera's prelude, but the music introducing this act is all about him. The G minor theme of its opening (a cousin to the love theme of the doomed Volsungs in *Die Walküre*) suddenly introduces a tone of melancholy that is basically absent from the lighthearted spirit of the first two acts. This theme represents an aspect of Sachs that he keeps hidden from the public. He discloses it unforgettably in his great "Wahn" monologue, which gives words to the theme (CD 1, track 7). In a concordance of Wagnerian terms, there would be a large entry for *Wahn*, one of his most frequently recurring thematic words. It's so packed with connotations that no simple equivalent works in English. *Wahn* (its leitmotif sounded at the opening by cellos and basses in B minor) entails a combination of illusion, madness, deception, and folly. Convoluted as Wagner's poetry here is—an attempt to imitate one of Shakespeare's great speeches

about the sway of madness over human affairs—the music clarifies its sudden shifts of emphasis.

Sachs (suddenly a good Schopenhauerian) laments the ubiq-
uity of *Wahn* in human nature (0:15): not even his beloved
Nuremberg is immune from its effects (2:03), as the riot of
the night before demonstrated (the violent music of 3:14 ff).
But the *Wahn* Sachs depicts is like a more humanistic version
of the Will pulsing through *Tristan*. Sachs gently recognizes its
role in bringing the young lovers together (3:53). *Wahn* even
plays a role in making sure Walther's art, like his love, attains
success: for such success cannot come about "without a touch of
madness" (5:47). Art itself, in other words, cannot escape the
circle of illusion. But it is a necessary illusion, one that allows
us to face life rather than be consumed by it in defeat. Wagner
conveys this complex web of thoughts again in a masterfully
immediate stroke later in the act. The audience is reminded that
Sachs too loves Eva. Yet Sachs renounces the chance to enjoy
this love and become part of the inevitable pattern that *Wahn*,
following human will, constantly replays.

The pattern even has its perfect point of reference, Sachs
suggests: the story of Tristan and Isolde. The orchestra then
directly quotes the chromatic, stepwise desire theme from
Wagner's *Tristan*. The message could hardly be clearer: illusory
as art is (that is, the "story of Tristan and Isolde"), it encodes
a wisdom that Sachs draws on to avoid a worse illusion: the
illusion that expressing his love for Eva could avoid replicating
Tristan's fatal pattern. And he goes further: he actually reclaims
the "foreign" sound of his *Tristan* music and integrates it as an
essential part of the quintet's fabric, drawing on the climax
of *Tristan*'s duet (as well as a quote again from the *Walküre*
love music).

Walther presents his latest inspiration to Sachs—it arrived,
unsurprisingly, in a dream—but his improvisation requires

shaping. David's comical attempt at schooling in act 1 had no impact. Now, however, Walther is willing to listen. Sachs clarifies the role of form in taming what would otherwise remain the impetuous art Walther introduced in his audition before the Mastersingers. Its emotional sincerity is not in question; but if no one can understand it, not even someone as willing as Sachs, what use is the art? Wagner manages to make an apparently esoteric topic in fact fascinating, dramatizing the evolution of Walther's "Prize Song" (CD 1, track 8) at the same time as he illustrates the basic AAB form underlying the master-song. This is the so-called *bar form:* it features two strophes to the same melody but with harmonic modulation (starting at 0:25 and 2:10, beginning "in the morning" and "in the evening," respectively). These are followed by a final strophe with an entirely new melody (3:44: the melody introduced in the *Meistersinger* prelude, climaxing on the tenor's high A at 4:55) that synthesizes elements of the former.

These aren't just pedantic explanations from Sachs. Rather, they serve as a parable of Wagner's own art. One danger of his focus on the drama for the artwork of the future was that it was perceived to unleash the musical setting, rendering it formless. Yet the composer's enthusiastic response to Schopenhauer brought back home to him the critical role played by music as a form of revelation. To communicate most effectively, music must be perceived within formal structures. The musicologist Alfred Lorenz even claimed to be able to decode repeated patterns of AAB throughout Wagner's work. Like any of the reductive tendencies imposed on his operas, such systems must always be regarded skeptically. But Lorenz's claim about *Die Meistersinger*'s own form has a fascinating logic: essentially, the entire opera replicates the AAB form on a vast scale with its three acts. The first two (AA) share a similarity of tone, with some variation, but it is act 3 that takes the opera to an entirely different level while resolving the conflicts in the first two (B). This in part explains the absence of Sachs from the prelude: he is the "new element" formed from what has come before.

This, as much as any psychological return to the past suggested above, lies behind the many "closed forms" of old-school opera contained within the score. Wagner develops larger complexes out of what are recognizable songs or set numbers onto themselves: Walther's audition music in act 1, Sachs's "Cobbler's Song," Beckmesser's (tellingly interrupted) serenade, the monologues of Sachs, the quintet, and of course the "Prize Song" as it evolves throughout the opera.

But the form must be flexible. It must be able to adapt to new content. Beckmesser makes a fool of himself not just because he mangles the poetry he has "borrowed" from Sachs: he attempts to fit it to his boring, unimaginative, archaic lute mode and so is doomed from the start. His denunciations of Walther at the beginning (motivated, the libretto points out, by jealousy) eerily anticipate the fossilized thinking of Stalinist—and Nazi—critics of modernism. Beckmesser is often described as a parody of Wagner's gadfly critic Eduard Hanslick (who had started his career as an admirer of the composer). The matter isn't so simple. There has been much attention lately to Beckmesser as a negative icon who transmits Wagner's virulent anti-Semitism directly into the opera. The debate about the extent to which the composer's most repulsive views actually infect his art continues to rage, and by its very nature, it can never be definitively settled.

Still, it would be disingenuous to ignore this issue as peripheral. The basic argument is that Beckmesser's high-pitched vocal setting and melismas (coming from a role specifically set for a bass-baritone voice) are meant to parody cantorial singing, even though Beckmesser is not explicitly identified as Jewish but in fact is an integral member of the Mastersingers

Guild. A range of commentators from Theodor Adorno to Marc Weiner has claimed that his singing, and his mangling of the verse at the Song Festival, actually illustrates Wagner's description of Jewish music in his notorious essay "Das Judentum in der Musik" (Judaism in Music)—and Wagner did, after all, choose to republish it in a revision the year after *Die Meistersinger*'s premiere. It's important to recognize that there is a darker aspect to *Die Meistersinger*, mostly concentrated in the treatment of Beckmesser, which makes the audience feel uncomfortable. The hapless Marker also shares something with Dickens's crueler caricatures and, even more, with the sadistic punishment meted out to Malvolio in *Twelfth Night*. What to make of these unsettling aspects is often a cornerstone of a production's overall interpretation of the opera.

Wagner himself seems aware in this opera of the underlying ugliness in life that is barely kept at bay. The act 2 riot-finale was a part of his first image for the work in the Sachs-Marker confrontation. He shows how quickly Nuremberg's delicate balance can be unsettled, allowing its peaceful utopia to boil over into violence and aggression. Sachs emphasizes the point when he reflects on it in his "Wahn" monologue of the following act (track 7, 3:29 ff). Walther shows a predisposition to violence in his frustrated state in act 2. And violence appears again in the warning of Sachs's final speech to the populace (violence here as a threat to Germany from without, to which the best defense is "holy German art"). This, along with Beckmesser's character, is the other great trouble-spot for those who want their *Meistersinger* to be only sunny and unequivocally humanistic. The chauvinism of Sachs's words, advising against "foreign" infiltration, is undeniable.

But the violence threatening Nuremberg is also the violence to which humanity is continually subject: the violence in fact that is the product of *Wahn* and from which not even the people gathered before Sachs are immune. The only hope, Sachs reminds them, is the truth offered by the kind of art they have just experienced in Walther's song. And that art is the product of all the tensions and conflicts the audience has participated in over the lengthy stretch of this "light-hearted comedy": innovation vs. tradition, the young vs. the old, spontaneous feeling vs. wise, reflective shaping. It isn't a question of either/or, of a single side of the equation winning out. Wagner's focus in *Die Meistersinger* is on art as mediating the balance between these conflicting forces: like the interplay of aggressive sea against yielding rock that is Emerson's image for progress. In a sense, the duty of each new era of interpreters to come to terms with the opera in its entirety—its humanism and its less savory aspects—mirrors the task of taking art seriously as outlined by *Die Meistersinger.*

Total Artistic Clarity
An Overview of the *Ring* Cycle

*Mark well my new poem: it contains the world's beginning
and its end.*

—Letter to Liszt

The *Ring* cycle stands apart: not just in Wagner's career nor in music and theater history alone for that matter. It stands apart within the entire context of artistic ambition since that turning point known as the Renaissance. Almost everything connected with it involves a paradigm shift. The *Ring*'s unprecedented duration (roughly fifteen hours of music, spread over four days) has a counterpart in Wagner's nearly three-decade-long obsession with the project from genesis to full execution. Moreover, his plan led to a vastly expanded role for the orchestra and a new approach to the poetry he developed for his texts. Extending beyond the work itself, the *Ring* encircles an ambit in which Wagner went so far as to reimagine an entire society. For the *Ring* was conceived not only as a radical departure from convention; to be realized properly, its creator also insisted that a new kind of performer, theater, and even audience would be necessary.

Yet for all its novelty, the *Ring* invokes the primal, mythic imagery of cosmic birth and death. Much of its impact relies on the familiar archetype, apocalyptic in scale, of change and renewal (examples include the overthrow of the Titans in Greek mythology or the cycles of the Hindu *Mahabharata*). Even the unifying symbolism of the ring that confers power is just one manifestation of an ancient and recurring morality tale. Plato's anecdote of the shepherd Gyges who discovers a corrupting ring, as recounted in *The Republic,* is an especially well-known version (which may in turn have provided the seed for the famous variant at the heart of J. R. R. Tolkien's *The Lord of the Rings*).

Such ancient and universal wisdom traditions, as refracted through the lens of Germanic mythology, are the deep structure onto which Wagner loaded his most urgent preoccupations. The *Ring* became Wagner's focal point during his most revolutionary phase. It was first of all to be a vehicle for his (always interconnected) dreams of political and artistic reform. But the *Ring* also served as a kind of sustaining Holy Grail for Wagner, a compendium of his changing philosophical and spiritual attitudes in grappling with the ultimate questions. Into it he poured his deepest intuitions, as expressed through ever-evolving artistic confidence. Wagner called the *Ring,* in a letter to Liszt, "the poem of my life and of all that I am and feel."

It's important to keep in mind that Wagner first gravitated toward the *Ring* in his prime, while a thirty-five-year-old man (in 1848, the halfway point of his life). The dream he began to nurture then wasn't fulfilled until he was sixty-three, when the *Ring* was performed for the first time as the intended complete cycle in 1876. This lengthy span of creation (exceeded only by *Parsifal*) partially accounts for the work's remarkably rich layering, as well as its internal contradictions. Many fascinating theories revolve around extrinsic circumstances—political disillusionment, the discovery of Schopenhauer, input from Wagner's intimate circle of friends—and their impact on the *Ring*. But ultimately the basic reality of living with his characters for so long and viewing them as a kind of mirror (and vice versa) must account for the shifting sensibilities at work as the *Ring* progresses. Wagner indeed saw the idea of change as integral to the work when he described it in a famous letter to his imprisoned friend August Röckel in January 1854. He summarized the *Ring* as being "concerned to show how necessary it is to acknowledge change, variety, multiplicity and the eternal newness of reality and of life, and to yield to that necessity."

Multiplicity is certainly to be found in the bewildering number of tributary sources that eventually flowed into the *Ring*'s mighty river. Tracking these down has, in itself, been the topic of many a book (a particularly in-depth contribution being Elizabeth Magee's *Richard Wagner and the Nibelungs*). Wagner gives his cycle the full title *Der Ring des Nibelungen* (The Ring of the Nibelung—referring to the character Alberich, not to the Nibelungs as a class), thereby pointing to the anonymous epic *Das Nibelungenlied*. This medieval German epic (given literary form around 1200) had been rediscovered in the surge of early German Romanticism. An influential music journal had in fact already suggested it as ripe material for a German national opera, with composers such as Mendelssohn and Schumann contemplating the challenge (and the now-forgotten Heinrich Dorn undertaking it in his opera *Die Nibelungen*).

Wagner seems finally to have warmed to the idea in the wake of *Lohengrin*. During the Dresden period, his voracious reading habits were fueled by access to the Royal Library. He began to amass a private collection of classics and Germanic lore (now housed at the Bayreuth Museum), including versions of the *Nibelungenlied*. But even at the start, it was clear that this epic couldn't in itself provide a sufficiently cogent source of inspiration. By October 1848, Wagner had drawn together an astonishing mixture of material in a prose scenario entitled

"Der Nibelungen-Mythus: als Entwurf zu einem Drama" (The Nibelung Myth as Sketch for a Drama).

In addition to the *Nibelungenlied,* this included other primary sources from German and Scandinavian mythology (chiefly the collections of Eddic poems and the *Volsunga Saga*). But Wagner's research also relied heavily on contemporary scholarship (and speculation), as well as early nineteenth-century Romantic fiction and the Grimm Brothers' collections of fairy tales.

Mining this material like a Nibelung himself, Wagner repeated the by-now-familiar pattern, but on a vastly grander scale than anywhere else in his work. He combined, improvised on, and simplified this Babel of sources (entailing a virtual encyclopedia of individual stories) to fashion a unified narration in his prose sketch. It became the nucleus for the *Ring.* Wagner's first idea, though, was for a single tragic opera called *Siegfrieds Tod* (Siegfried's Death), focused on the climax of the story and the central *Nibelungenlied* characters Siegfried and Brünnhilde—the basis for what became *Götterdämmerung* (Twilight of the Gods). He drafted a libretto just a month after the sketch (in November 1848). In her study of *Parsifal,* Lucy Beckett observes how Wagner's imagination often fixated on powerful stage visuals as his works began to take shape. She points to the image of Siegfried's murder and dead body being carried from the stage as the original kernel of inspiration from which the *Ring* germinated.

This tale of betrayal and tragic downfall, followed by Brünnhilde's redeeming sacrifice, held profound significance for Wagner. To him it encoded a core of mythic truth about the timeless conflict between love and the will to power. Above all it seemed to mirror the inherent evil of contemporary society and yet to represent the hope of revolutionary change. But all these ideas were still too abstract in the *Siegfrieds Tod* setting. Or rather, they depended on lengthy, inert stretches of narrative. Following the interruption of the actual, but abortive, Revolution in Dresden in 1849 that resulted in his exile, Wagner spent a great deal of time mulling over his material. He also vented his frustrated revolutionary fervor in a series of crucial theoretical writings: *Die Kunst und die Revolution* (Art and Revolution), *Das Kunstwrk der Zukunft* (The Artwork of the Future), and most consequentially, *Oper und Drama* (Opera and Drama).

All of these projects were Wagner's method of wrestling with his desires for cultural reform and specifically with the Nibelung idea, which he was convinced required a radical pathway different from the solutions he had found in his previous operas. Before he could clear the way for that, he needed to come to grips on a theoretical level with the issues involved: how to return art to serious political and social relevance and how to construct from drama and music an organic unity that would communicate fully with the audience. Wagner actually began some musical sketches for *Siegfrieds Tod,* but nothing seemed to take flight. During this period, as Wagner adjusted to exile in Zurich, the composer incubated his plans amid long hiking tours in the Alps and elaborate hydrotherapy treatments.

The act of writing *Lohengrin* had deepened Wagner's respect for the potential of myth. For one thing, with its clash of legendary and historical aspects, it pointed a way beyond the conventions of the plot-driven, by-the-numbers historical grand opera then in vogue. The formulaic successes crowding the stage exemplified the latter (Wagner's critiques thereof sound a lot like contemporary detractors of the commercial film industry's emptiness). *Lohengrin,* moreover, seemed to embody core truths precisely because of its mythic qualities, in a way Wagner was convinced offered greater clarity and accessibility.

His focus on myth notwithstanding, Wagner never entirely abandoned historical subjects. *Die Meistersinger,* as discussed, remained a creative goal that he eventually realized. During the early period of the *Ring* genesis, he was still considering a number of projects based on historical figures (including even a spoken drama on the Holy Roman Emperor and Crusader Frederick Barbarossa, whom Wagner bizarrely fantasized as a figure parallel to the mythic Siegfried). But in general he was drawing closer to the distinction made famous in Aristotle's *Poetics:* tragedy (based on myth) is a higher and more universal form than history. Not that Wagner was by any means a conventional Aristotelian. He was deeply suspicious of pure rationalism; Wagnerian catharsis is meant to be an experience more shattering than Aristotle's essentially medical notion.

Yet the classical world exerted a profound sway over Wagner and, specifically, over the *Ring.* His autobiography recalls the enormous pleasure of reading Aeschylus in his garden as he took breaks from composing *Lohengrin.* Aside from any dramaturgical necessity, the *Ring*'s expansion has in part to do with models from the trilogies of Athenian tragedy: the *Oresteia* and the Prometheus and Oedipus cycles (Wagner conceived the *Ring* as a trilogy, *Das Rheingold* serving as a prelude). Many considered the *Nibelungenlied* a kind of Germanic *Iliad,* with the same kind of potential to supply material for tragic drama as Homeric epic did for the classical tragedians. Wagner's theorizing about the union of the arts in the artwork of the future was, after all, based on an idealized fantasy of a lost golden age of art in classical Athens. His model for the *Gesamtkunstwerk* (literally, the "total art work" as a synthesis of drama, music, poetry, dance, visuals—in fact all aspects of the performing arts) emerged from this fantasy as an antidote to the depressing specialization he observed about him, which he perceived as nothing more than masturbatory art, a vapid display of effects for the sake of effects.

Wagner wanted to recapture that presumed union in the *Ring:* not in the sense of a Renaissance, but rather as a radically new form that took advantage of the subsequent evolution of drama and music (epitomized by Shakespeare and Beethoven, respectively).

Moreover, the idea that became Bayreuth derived from Wagner's admiration for the communal aspect of ancient Greek theater, which was presented at special festivals. For Wagner, this symbolized an enviable recognition of art's essential social function, as opposed to considering it mere entertainment. These were some of the ideas that would originally attract Nietzsche, a maverick classical philologist turned philosopher, to the Wagnerian cause.

Another crucial influence from the classical world was the widespread nineteenth-century notion of "Hellenic optimism" (Nietzsche, ironically influenced by Wagner, would do much to dispel this stereotype in delving into the shadow side of ancient Greece). The Greek declaration that "man is the measure of all things" was seen as a proud rebellion against ancient super-stition. During the *Ring*'s early gestation, Wagner subscribed to the humanist, materialist philosophy of Ludwig Feuerbach. Feuerbach's deconstruction of religion as basically an anthro-pomorphic projection of human ideals profoundly influenced Wagner's original attraction to the interplay between gods and humans in the *Ring* myth. The overthrow of the gods there-fore becomes a necessary evolutionary step for fully human liberation to take place. These ideas will coexist with his subsequent adoption of Schopenhauer's diametrically opposed philosophy of resignation, creating a fascinating tension in the *Ring* as a whole.

In bringing together the vastly disparate material of the original 1848 Nibelung sketch, Wagner's great insight had been to link the Siegfried tragedy with the myths of the gods and their cycle of destruction in a clear line of cause and effect. This gave the core myth of *Siegfrieds Tod* a profoundly more significant context and resonance. Even more, it was essential to connect intimately the parallel universes of gods and humans. Wagner's early, revolution-inspired scheme depended on this contrast between the old order of gods and heroes who strive to liberate the corrupt world they have inherited.

But interweaving them conceptually via chunks of narrative wasn't enough. What went wrong under the old gods is merely described in the original *Siegfrieds Tod* opera. Wagner's letters detail the process of dramaturgical reflection that led him to expand on it. In the summer of 1851, he decided to pair the tragedy with a complementary, comic treatment of the hero's early exploits called *Der junge Siegfried,* which was later renamed simply *Siegfried.* Wagner's impulse was to "imprint" such deeds as the slaying of the dragon and the waking of Brünnhilde with "sharply defined physical images...so that by the time they hear the more serious Siegfried's Death, the audience will know all the things that are taken for granted or simply hinted at there."

Feedback from close friends with whom Wagner shared his plans resulted in expanding the work into two more operas based on the events leading up to Siegfried's life. *Die Walküre* (The Valkyrie) concerns itself with his parents and the earlier role of Brünnhilde and her father Wotan, head of the old order of gods. To this he added *Das Rheingold* (The Rhinegold), introducing the fable of the treasure and cursed ring that ultimately ensure Siegfried's tragic death. Wagner completed the texts for these last two by the fall of 1852. He then revised those he had written earlier, gathered them together, and published all four in a private edition early in 1853. Wagner had by then settled on the title *Der Ring des Nibelungen* for the entire cycle. He subtitled the work "A Stage Festival Play for Three Days and a Preliminary Evening."

The intriguing fact that Wagner wrote the librettos in reverse order shouldn't be overemphasized. It only underscores how thoroughly intermingled had become this idiosyncratic array of mythic sources, recast according to his imagination. Often this aspect of the *Ring's* genesis is presented as a simple matter of fleshing out the "exposition," like a series of Hollywood pre-quels. That's a ridiculous simplification of the matter. In his classic *Ring* commentary *The Perfect Wagnerite,* George Bernard Shaw astutely points out that the expansion was necessary to clarify the dramatic stakes in setting up the conflict between old and new represented by Siegfried's story. Wagner himself explains his artistic intuition: "a work of art—and hence the basic drama—can only make its rightful impression if the poetic intent is fully represented to the senses in every one of its important moments": showing, that is, vastly excels telling. "In order to be perfectly understood, I must therefore communicate my entire myth, in its deepest and widest significance, with total artistic clarity."

Possibly the single factor in the *Ring's* makeup most often viewed as impeding that clarity is the peculiar linguistic approach Wagner developed for his librettos. One of the delightful surprises of his research into the Eddas and similar material was the discovery of *Stabreim:* a kind of intensely alliterative verse based on stressed syllables. A well-known related example is the poetry of the Old English epic *Beowulf.* Wagner's impulse to theorize extended to everything, including linguistic theory, and he grew excited over the (mistaken) assumption that such verse was a relic of a golden age of more musical human speech. For his *Ring* texts, Wagner developed a *Stabreim* system of his own, for the most part abandoning the classical meter and rhymed couplets of his previous librettos.

Wagner's attempts to re-create *Stabreim* result in a weirdly pseudo-archaic tone with frequently convoluted expressions. The omnipresence of the alliterative style has been mercilessly satirized since the *Ring*'s premiere. But despite all of its absurdities, Wagner's *Stabreim* does allow him to flex his considerable philological muscle through thematic word echoes that form a sort of counterpart to the musical web of recurrent motives. His implied associations of words via alliteration take a number of forms, including incessant punning and etymological suggestiveness.

Why did this material exercise such magnetism over Wagner in the first place? When he completed *Lohengrin* in the spring of 1848, the Revolution that would spread through Europe was gathering steam. Wagner had now been in his position as Kapellmeister in Dresden for six years. But even its security and steady income could hardly distract him from suffocating desperation. With painful clarity, the divide between his artistic desires and the unbudging status quo continued to sharpen. The composer's far-reaching proposals to his bosses outlining serious orchestral and theater reform fell on deaf ears. Wagner had lost faith in trying to reform the institutions from within; there seemed to be little point in churning out new works for the old system, which for the composer meant nothing but claptrap and frivolous entertainment.

He had meanwhile become close friends with his assistant conductor August Röckel, a composer himself. Röckel edited a radical journal and helped inspire Wagner's enthusiasm for the Revolutionists. By the time the Revolution reached Dresden, Wagner was in league with Röckel and the famous Russian anarchist Mikhail Bakunin. His retrospective accounts hedge and downplay his role in the actual riots, but there's evidence that Wagner was in the thick of it. A legend even spread that he was involved in the burning of the old opera house, which, however apocryphal an image, contains a certain poetic irony.

The Revolution failed. Harsh reactionary measures followed. Wagner hightailed it first to his friend Liszt in Weimar and then barely eluded capture on his way into the exile that would last until the 1860s. His associates weren't so lucky: Röckel and Bakunin were both taken by the authorities. After the harrowing news that his dear friend Röckel had been given a death sentence, Wagner was relieved to learn it had been commuted to a lengthy prison term. Some of the composer's most lucid comments on the *Ring* appear in the course of the letters he wrote to Röckel, who apparently had the gumption to challenge Wagner's project with perceptive questions and critiques.

Wagner's exile only heightened his sense of revolutionary purpose—as applied to his art, that is. There was now no turning back. This was the period when the *Ring* was expanding into a project of gigantic dimensions (Wagner originally suggested a timeline of just three years needed to complete the music). Along with his ideas of the *Ring* as artistic reform, Wagner contemplated the special performing conditions it would require. This was the epitome of his belief that art can change society. However polar Bertolt Brecht seems as an opposite to Wagner, this is exactly the same impulse of engaged art informing his own revolutionary theater. It's the recurrent desire for a kind of art that can influence one's life, which again came to the fore, say, in the 1960s.

Indeed, Wagner's fantasies of a transfiguring festival in a temporary theater (at one point he even imagined it on the banks of the Mississippi), which would occur just once and subsequently be burnt, almost prefigure Woodstock. Eventually, of course, his fixation on the unique performance conditions needed to bring the *Ring* off properly would be concretely realized in his own Bayreuth Theater. Wagner was forced, against his will, to allow preliminary productions in Munich of *Das Rheingold* and *Die Walküre,* due to King Ludwig's insistence. But the entire cycle was first unveiled as a unity in Bayreuth's inaugural season during August 1876.

It's astounding enough that Wagner found a way to pull all these strands of influence together into a unified dramatic scheme. But even more stunning is the breakthrough that enabled Wagner to conceive and actually execute a reinforcing musical unity. Hand in hand with his theatrical instincts, Wagner developed an overarching musical system with the necessary power and flexibility to bind this entire imagined world together. As will be seen, Wagner's deployment of his leitmotif theory provides a brilliantly effective matrix of variation and recombination against which the *Ring* unfolds. But that is far from Wagner's only strategy for achieving musical coherence. His integration of text and musical setting, increasingly bold harmonic imagination, use of polyphony, and approach to tonality and orchestral coloration are each of paramount significance.

In the end, Wagner's discovery of the *Ring* material proved to be the turning point in his artistic development. It led to an internal revolution far more profound and lasting than the external one that was merely a catalyst. Wagner devoted an enormous amount of his career to working out the implications of this artistic bonanza. The result—which will now be examined in greater depth—was an artwork of inexhaustible richness, which over a lifetime continues to yield new discoveries.

Shimmering Enigmas
Das Rheingold

We take the *Ring* for granted. But it's hard to fathom how intimidating it must have seemed to plunge into its actual composition. After years of thinking about it, Wagner had staked out immense proportions for his project by the time he had all four *Ring* poems printed together in February 1853. Moreover, during that period he had channeled his energies into a hefty amount of theorizing about how opera should be reformed. *Lohengrin* was the last significant piece of music he had completed. Aside from some tentative sketches for the *Ring* and a couple of minor piano pieces, Wagner was coming out of a musical hibernation of nearly six years when he began to compose again in earnest by undertaking *Das Rheingold* in late 1853.

The composer's famous "vision" at La Spezia in Italy in which he dreamt the music to open his cycle, previously recounted in the *Meistersinger* discussion, may be one of his many fanciful spins. Regardless, it's a colorful reminder of Wagner's frequent assertion that he couldn't hurry the process of inspiration but had to wait on its own terms. Once he made his first breakthrough into the *Ring,* however, the music for *Rheingold* indeed came in a torrent (working out the unusual orchestration his *Ring* required would be a more cumbersome matter). Wagner sketched out his first draft of the complete opera between

November 1, 1853, and January 14, 1854, and finished the fully orchestrated score that September.

However long his dry spell had lasted, ideas obviously were ripening all along in the composer's restless subconscious. *Das Rheingold* belongs to that class of creative leaps that are so rare as to seem miraculous. Other examples would be Beethoven's "Eroica" Symphony, Mahler's First Symphony, or the Stravinsky of *The Rite of Spring*. Any assumption that *Das Rheingold* is merely about exposition—because it presents the "back story" of the ring and its curse as well as several key musical motives for the first time—is misguided. Wagner exercises a sense of newfound prowess in this score. Its extraordinary surges of vitality and harnessed energy announce a brave new world, ushering his audience with confidence into the heart of Wagner's unprecedented epic journey.

The very opening is a potent realization in sound of emergence, of becoming as a process. The prelude to *Das Rheingold* represents the epitome of Wagner's obsession with origins. This desire to trace things back as far as possible informs his attempt to strip away detailed stories to their mythic core. It might also be seen in his fascination with etymology. Of course, the *Ring*'s own origin can be ascribed in part to this impulse to follow the story back to its starting point. But nowhere is Wagner's preoccupation so graphic as in his sonic depiction of the very beginning of time in this prelude (CD 2, track 1). In contrast to the unsettling sense of chaos electrified into form that Beethoven paints at the beginning of his Ninth Symphony, Wagner's musical Genesis is one of stasis, mesmerizing in its very monotony. The basses intone a long E-flat, which seems to sound without pulse (0:01); to this is added its dominant (B-flat) on top in the bassoons. Together these two notes—the systole and diastole of Western tonality—carve out a drone-like *naked fifth* (a hollowed-out triad, made of just the tonic

and dominant, with no third; 0:08). (It's intriguing to compare Wagner's choice of E-flat—the home key of Beethoven's
Eroica—with recent observations by astrophysicists: apparently
the oldest known "note" in the universe is in the universe is a
B-flat frequency [the dominant of E-flat] emitted from a black
hole in the Perseus galaxy.)

This hollow, persistent fifth forms the ground from which
eight horns, subtly interlaced in a roundlike chain of repetitions, give forth the *Ring* cycle's very first leitmotif (starting
at 0:30). Wagner's genius here is to build up a subtle tension
between the restful stasis of the beginning and the process of
change, of coming to be. This indeed announces one of the
fundamental tensions structuring the entire cycle (akin to the
Freudian pull between *thanatos* [death] and *eros* [love]). Wagner
accomplishes this by showing his theme to evolve through a
kind of time-lapse. First we hear the cellos in a faster, evenly
flowing, scalar tracing of the theme (1:30) and then they double
their speed as the clarinets transform the theme into its more
definitive statement (2:24). This primal theme will be associated variously with innocent nature, water (specifically, the
primordial Rhine), and even evolution itself.

Wagner may even have incorporated the *golden mean*—the
so-called divine proportion prized by Pythagoras and used by
Renaissance artists to structure paintings. If one considers the
ratio of the entire prelude's length to the time elapsed when the
definitive statement of the nature motive emerges, the result is
too close to this classical ratio (approximately 1.6) to be a coincidence (in most performances, in any case). Wagner continues
to add density to the orchestration as he increases volume in a
gradual, prolonged crescendo. The swirling textures of sound
readily transmit the idea of water rushing and complement
the music's quickening into life. All this Wagner accomplishes
almost imperceptibly, for the entire prelude has taken place

without a change from the key of E-flat. Not only was this a radical strategy in the context of his time (as radical as atonality, of which it is the opposite, if you will); many have noted the uncanny premonition here of the minimalist aesthetic.

It will be helpful to dwell just a bit longer on *Rheingold*'s prelude, for it is in many senses a germinal moment in the musical texture of the entire *Ring*. The prelude doesn't simply provide an ideal entrée into the composer's mythic landscape. Rather, it introduces the very concept of motivic generation, growth, and fragmentation. The very opening musical idea unfurls a sequence of notes from the basic E-flat triad—a *broken chord* in musicological jargon—moving upward (that is, "becoming"). By simply breaking up the triad into unique patterns, Wagner creates an entire class of fundamental motives, such as those for the Rhinegold, the Valkyries, or the heroically liberating sword. Please note that such labeling is simply a linguistic stepping stone; the essential inadequacy of these labels, it is hoped, is one of the chief points of this discussion. Motives are also formed by adding melodic passage-notes to this broken chord: for instance, nature, the Rhinemaidens, Siegfried's horn call, and Valhalla. Still more groups of motives grow from mere intervals, others from scalar passages (for example, Wotan's Spear), and yet others from combinations of all of these (Brünnhilde as woman).

Meanwhile, as legions of commentators have observed, motives are linked together as families by associated musical and dramatic ideas (sometimes even as opposites). The result is a fascinating field of ambivalence in which an individual motive gains a larger significance by association with another motive derived from its "family." For example, when given in the minor, the nature motive emerges as the signature of Erda, the Earth Mother. And here's what a change of direction can do: Erda's music in reverse completes the cycle of becoming and represents the downfall of the gods (with all its associations of resignation, fate, and so forth). It also shares its descending plunge with Wotan's Spear.

Robert Donington's justly admired Jungian take on the cycle (*Wagner's Ring and Its Symbols*) presents one of the most sensible of the many attempts to devise a taxonomy for the *Ring*'s leitmotifs. He suggests various ways of grouping and cross-associating them. His most significant insight with regard to musical organization is how the leitmotifs interrelate within constantly shifting contexts. Donington shows how they form a network of *developing* meaning, not a closed, fixed system. His account of their connections is beautifully aligned with the psychological symbolism he is most interested in exploring. Indeed, as one gains familiarity with the *Ring,* the practice of simply labeling leitmotifs becomes increasingly superfluous, if not outright misleading.

However one decides to interpret the drama unfolding, this musical network is what lends the *Ring* its unique identity as an organically varied and complex yet unified web (the image is Wagner's), interlocking symphonic goals with dramatic ones. The composer's excitement at his breakthrough in the prelude was about figuring out how to begin. But it also must have included exhilaration over realizing what Carl Dahlhaus calls "the possibility of deriving a motivic universe from a single idea." In *Richard Wagner's Music Dramas,* Dahlhaus notes the composer's epiphany as "the idea of developing the multitude of motives he needed from a small number of primal motives." Wagner, in other words, had discovered a magnificent system that he could use to generate musical structure so as to reinforce his vast dramatic structure. And its very flexibility gave him the freedom he needed not to feel bound by the straightjacket of his theory. This system engenders an immensely varied, many-layered trove of possible meanings, just as the emotional resonance of the work in turn constantly fluctuates. Every listener who returns to Wagner can attest to the phenomenon of ongoing personal discoveries, no matter how numerous previous encounters have been.

Wagner, for all his enthusiasm about the "intuitive truths" of original mythic sources, in fact devises his own myth of original sin in *Das Rheingold.* His invented story of the Nibelung dwarf Alberich's thwarted seduction of the Rhinemaidens might seem a passing incident before he illustrates the greed for power taking precedence. Yet the scene unfolds in a way that makes it pivotal. Alberich is led to his fateful decision to curse love and make the "avenging" ring from the gold he steals precisely because of their behavior. Especially before his discovery of Schopenhauer, Wagner espoused a very down-to-earth, even Freudian view of sexual love as "the real thing":

> But the full reality of love is possible only between the sexes: only as man and woman can we human beings really love, whereas all other forms of love are mere derivatives of it, originating in it, related to it or an unnatural imitation of it. It is wrong to regard this love as only one manifestation of love in general, and to assume that other and higher forms must therefore exist alongside it.

The cruel pleasure taken by the Rhinemaidens in thwarting this natural desire results in the "blowback" of Alberich's choice. Nature, it seems, isn't entirely innocent. In his classic, characteristically opinionated *Ring* commentary *The Perfect Wagnerite,* George Bernard Shaw observes the tragic ease with which the "golden age" can be supplanted by the "Plutonic" power of wealth once we turn away from love "and all the fruitful, creative, life-pursuing activities into which the loftiest human energy can develop it."

Yet Alberich's choice to foreswear love for the gold isn't the only "original sin" in the *Ring*. A marvelous example of Wagner's musico-dramatic web of associations relates this in the music that follows. Once Alberich has snatched the gold and let loose the narrative momentum, the first of the cycle's great orchestral scene changes is heard. The music of the watery depths graphically ascends into the Olympian heights of the gods, creating a link between these distant spheres as part of a unified world. But most striking is the obsessive insertion of the ring leitmotif.

Its writhing and indeterminate shape gradually metamorphoses via the horns into softer, more harmonious contours. Finally, at the beginning of the second scene, the full Valhalla motive is unveiled. Wagner actually allows the audience to hear the "ring" motive, with all its implications of illicit and corrupting power, *evolving* into the music associated with Wotan and the entire order of gods. From its first statement, so gloriously announced by the full panoply of Wagnerian brass, its very choralelike "solidity" is under question. The motive seems to be the model of diatonic stability, reaffirming the basic triad at the core of the *Ring* in the three fundamental chords of standard harmony. Yet we've already heard, by proximity, how closely its shape echoes the fluid motive of the ring. The rest of the opera explores and clarifies precisely this questionability—from the giants' demand for payment through the tricking of Alberich and the curse on the ring. The foundation of Wotan's power, however enlightened a ruler he wishes to be, is flawed at its core. The god himself will later draw attention to the parallels we hear in the music, referring to himself as "Licht Alberich" (Light Alberich) as opposed to "Schwarz Alberich" (Dark Alberich—that is, the dwarf in his full tyrannical power). Wotan has been far luckier in love than the dwarf, yet he has not found fulfillment: "whoever lives loves change and variety," he notes in defending his philandering to Fricka.

Wotan's first face-to-face confrontation with Alberich in the dwarf's home turf of Nibelheim itself is fascinating, for his revulsion seems based in part on self-recognition. Wotan too seems willing to sacrifice all to his power lust, in league with the cunning of Loge. The fire god's name is linked (in one of Wagner's fanciful pseudo-etymologies) with lying, for he also does duty as the god of reason, which in the *Ring*'s context means a tricky, lawyerlike sophistry. In the musical sphere, Loge's related motives all share an intensely chromatic, nervous character. Their half-step cascades and flickering trills function as an ambiguous, chromatic counterpart to the diatonic predictability of Valhalla and many other *Ring* motives. Yet Loge also represents a primal, natural force of energy that Wotan has succeeded in taming for his purposes.

Shaw's *The Perfect Wagnerite* admits a particular affection for *Das Rheingold*. The opera is, after all, the cornerstone for his interpretation of the *Ring* cycle as a socialist allegory of the inhumanity of industrial capitalism. Shaw especially delights in its lack of a traditional love story (love here is marked by its absence) and boldness in presenting "gloomy, ugly music" to depict the wretchedness of Alberich's slave workers in Nibelheim as a mirror of the sorry condition that has become "the way of the world" under capitalism. His reading was in turn a basis for the once iconoclastic, now legendary centennial production at Bayreuth by Patrice Chéreau with Pierre Boulez conducting, in which the Rhine is a hydroelectric dam and Wotan an imperious businessman trying to cope with foreclosure on the Valhalla mortgage.

Shaw's approach entails an idiosyncratic emphasis on the earlier part of the *Ring* as opposed to its climax. The beginning of the cycle meshes very nicely with the end, however, in productions that spotlight the prominent role nature plays throughout. There are many angles to work from here, without imposing a single-minded environmentalist interpretation—although, to be sure, Wagner's connection of natural catastrophe (through flood and fire) with the disaster of a civilization sick at its core can seem impressively prophetic. The Seattle Opera's production of 2001 became widely heralded as the "green *Ring*" for its emphasis on nature's deep-rooted significance in the cycle. Its scenic details are so lovingly fine-tuned one would scarcely be surprised to witness intrepid backpackers emerging from the old-growth forest beyond which Valhalla looms.

Indeed nature returns at the end of *Das Rheingold*—in the form of Erda's warning, instilling in Wotan a sudden desire for wisdom. But her appearance offers only a temporary reprieve from the snowballing curse. Along with Erda comes a sudden change in musical atmosphere, a brief premonition of the far different attitude that will be encountered in *Götterdämmerung*. The curse then effects its first murder (the Cain-and-Abel-like scene between the giants Fasolt and Fafner). After this somber context, the music returns to the protominimalist, sublime simplicity of the prelude, with Donner's storm-summoning and Froh's ensuing "Rainbow Bridge Ode" (CD 2, track 2, beginning). Yet even a reassuring restatement of the Valhalla music (0:24) cannot dispel the new sense of unease in such a freshly corrupted world (aside from the first scene, all of the events of the opera have taken place in a single day). Wotan begins (1:05) to declare his pride in the "shining fortress," but the element of anxiety, which will play so crucial a role henceforth, interrupts, morphing Valhalla back into the ring motive (1:51).

Here Wagner employs one of his most extraordinary leitmotif introductions. With a grandly portentous flourish, we hear a new motive (2:31), seemingly out of nowhere but connected to the composer's vague stage direction that Wotan must seem "resolute, as if seized by a great thought." In the opera to follow, this motive becomes more definitively associated with Siegmund's sword. But that is merely a symbol for the "great thought"—i.e., that Wotan still envisions a means to redeem the world through the agency of an uncorrupted hero. For now, he pockets the idea and allows himself the luxury of believing in what can only be a transient security. Loge's flickering music (4:18) underscores this transience, its flames already licking away at Valhalla's foundations. But most damning is the lament of the Rhinemaidens (4:42 ff), who proclaim their "truth" from the depths, while "false and craven is all that rejoices above." In the final measures, the simple theme of the rainbow bridge (like the prelude, generated from simple broken chords) blares with a monstrous grandiosity (7:01) in one of Wagner's brilliantly ironic moments: a hollow glory haloing the shimmering enigma that is Valhalla.

The Heart of the Matter
Die Walküre

Faced with a desert-island choice of just one opera from the *Ring,* the majority would likely vote for *Die Walküre.* This "first day of the stage festival play" as Wagner calls it—*Das Rheingold* being considered a "preliminary evening"—offers the most welcoming entrée into the cycle's labyrinthine vastness. The composer himself had particular affection for *Die Walküre.* Its opening love story brings the *Ring* into the human sphere for the first time (Siegmund and Sieglinde, as Wotan's offspring, are technically half divine, but they live entirely as mortals). And the reverberations of that story cast the gods themselves in a more human light, disclosing their deeper vulnerability. Psychological intensity pervades the entire work, inviting the audience in through the possibility of keen self-identification.

In contrast to the episodic scene changes of *Das Rheingold, Die Walküre* portrays its characters in much fuller dimension, exploring their inner lives and passions. Enriching the drama is an undercurrent from classical Greek tragedy. This is one of the many influences Wagner has digested into the texture of his *Ring*—to the point of shaping its outline as a trilogy (with a prelude). Alberich's curse from *Das Rheingold* now truly acquires a kind of doom-ridden omnipresence reminiscent of that marking the House of Atreus in the *Oresteia,* while the pull of fate holds sway throughout all three of *Die Walküre*'s acts. In *Opera and Drama,* Wagner reveals an affinity for Antigone. Clearly he models aspects of Brünnhilde's nobly defiant dis-obedience of law and authority on this tragic heroine from Sophocles' Oedipus cycle. Meanwhile, a classical sensibility informs his structuring of the drama almost entirely into a series of two-character dialogues (which continues in *Siegfried,* but only occurs intermittently in *Götterdämmerung*).

As with *Das Rheingold,* Wagner drafted the music for this (far longer) opera in a blaze of creativity, between June and December 1854. He completed the full orchestration in March 1856. As one will recall from *Tristan und Isolde,* this period encompasses the spiritual crisis during which Wagner discov-ered both the philosophy of Schopenhauer and the idea for his "monument" to love—the latter eventually compelling him to set aside his work on the *Ring.* This is also when he developed his friendship with the Wesendoncks and began to fall in love with Mathilde as his own marriage to Minna unraveled even further. Wagner had, of course, written the libretto of *Die Walküre* prior to these events. Yet, as an example of how tricky Wagnerian chronology can be, it's possible to sense the com-poser incorporating their emotional resonance into his full musical realization.

Die Walküre begins (like its predecessor) with a sonic depic-tion of nature. Yet the nature of the *Rheingold* prelude is more conceptual; here, it's concretized into the urgency of storm music. From this point through the rest of the cycle, several of the gods previously seen on stage retreat into the score itself, only to recur within the musical web (in this case, Donner and Froh). More incisively, the storm music functions simultane-ously as outer and inner nature. It quickly morphs into a figure for the stressful state of Siegmund, one of Wagner's outsider figures constantly on the run. Indeed this double-entrendre sense of storm recurs as a verbal motive and structures all of *Die Walküre:* Wotan jokes in act 2 about the "old storm" approaching in the figure of Fricka, while the "Ride of the Valkyries" opening the final act is the prelude to the storm of Wotan's wrath.

The first act focuses the audience's attention on the plight of characters who are minor from the *Ring*'s larger perspective (the opera's title, referring to Brünnhilde, indicates that Wotan's sphere is still the main concern). Yet Wagner brings them to life with such heartfelt eloquence that their scenes linger in the memory as among the most moving of the entire cycle. Siegmund and Sieglinde together actually *show* us for the first time the transforming effect of love—and, by extension, what is at stake when love is foresworn for the power represented by the ring. Even their love, it turns out, is doomed to exist as a merely transient interlude when set against the negative forces of the *Ring*'s universe. Indeed, it sets the pattern for such transience. It is seen again in the cycle's other principal illustrations of the redeeming power of love: that between Wotan and his daughter Brünnhilde (from whom he must separate) and the love of Brünnhilde and Siegfried (quickly unraveled by the climactic intrigues of *Götterdämmerung*).

It's a truism that love in opera happens at first sight. This is especially true in Wagner (think of Senta and the Dutchman or Elsa and Lohengrin, notwithstanding their predictive dreams). What's so remarkable about this love story is how persuasively and knowingly he depicts the actual *process* of falling in love. This isn't precisely love at first sight—Siegmund and Sieglinde are reunited, having been separated as small children—but Wagner takes pains to emphasize the role of meaningful gazes they share (the gaze will recur as an important feature in sealing the love of Tristan and Isolde). Their exchanges in fact echo the familiar sense lovers have of already knowing each other when they first fall in love. Most movingly, the music seems to expose exactly what is going on inside and between them (CD 2, track 3). The orchestra tenderly embroiders the motives associated with each (Siegmund at 0:08 and Sieglinde at 1:28) into a symphonically intricate pattern as Sieglinde offers water to her guest (2:24 ff). Robert Donington observes: "There is no lovelier moment in the *Ring* than the seven bars here compounded of an inspired expansion of their motives.... Water so yearned for as this may well symbolize the water of life, for which she is becoming a channel for him."

How astonishing to realize that all this time, Wagner is following his principles of integration between music and text. *Die Walküre* in fact adheres quite strictly to the ideas of *Opera and Drama,* displaying an even greater confidence in them than *Das Rheingold.* Even at the height of their passion, the lovers are not allowed to mingle words together. And in this introductory scene, what would have once been set as standard-issue recitative acquires beautiful nuance, always attuned to the natural rhythm and accent of the speech (e.g., 0:43 ff). Yet Wagner brilliantly disguises his artifice. Instead, he conveys a feeling of genuine spontaneity, particularly in the musical birth of the Volsungs' love, which is first proclaimed by a solo cello, supported by strings (3:00).

Its eloquence is overpowering, a microcosm of what Donington calls "the almost unbelievable poignancy and lyrical perfection of the first Act...due as much as anything to the mastery with which the bitterness of pain and the sweetness of love are blended." Yet even this theme, soon fragmented into components that are constantly woven into the fabric of the act, derives from the leitmotif system. Its basic contour has already been encountered in a more hectic version in *Das Rheingold* as the music of Freia, goddess of love (and of the golden apples that preserve the gods' youthfulness). Indeed, a new level of psychological resonance attaches to the leitmotifs by virtue of the changed context. For example, Wotan's proud Valhalla theme gains poignancy when heard during Sieglinde's narration (telling the audience what the characters don't know about the identity of the twins' father).

This first scene between Siegmund and Sieglinde is also a splendid case of the sensitivity of Wagner's orchestration (and a good rejoinder to the cliché that his music is always loud and blaring). His subtle blend of tone colors has a chamber-music-like intimacy. It renders the full wash of orchestral sonority in the final scene's love duet even more effective, a sonic counterpart to the moonlight flooding hope briefly into their lives. Wagner makes prominent use of pauses in this act, foreshadowing his pregnant use of silence in the "Death Annunciation" scene of act 2 and in the final confrontation between Wotan and his daughter. The music for the transition to Siegmund's solo monologue contains some of Wagner's signature tension-building techniques, which will recur prominently in *Götterdämmerung.* Quite possibly inspired by the scherzo music of Beethoven's Fifth Symphony, Wagner exploits sustained pianissimos and somber colors in the nether regions of the orchestra accompanied by timpani. These pauses seem to represent the characters in the act of taking in what is transpiring, and this adds to the inwardness of the opera as a whole, in contrast to the "extroverted" character of much of *Das Rheingold.*

The warmth and humanity of this love story form a glowing oasis within the severity of the world depicted in the *Ring.* But it is tellingly brief. Hunding's music brutally intersects it. His presence reminds us that this is a society where love is a luxury and women are given the status of property. Hunding's motive, with its jabbing chords and arresting rhythms, shares its haughty barbarism with that of the Giants (those hammering chords will recur at the very moment of Siegfried's death and be integrated into his Funeral March).

As an aside, Hunding is one of those characters who pose a difficulty for interpreters seeking to define Alberich and Mime as the only source of evil in the cycle—and more pointedly, as nothing but incorporations of Wagner's anti-Semitism. Hunding is, after all, the very image of the tribal "Volk" and actually does receive more or less two-dimensional treatment. In the *Ring*'s moral universe, he is decidedly a negative force as an unthinking supporter of blind convention. In fact, Wagner wastes no pity on him: he's one of the few characters from the *Ring* the audience is quite happy to see dispatched when he finally meets his fate. But Alberich and Mime are far too richly characterized to be reduced to a black-and-white ideological scheme.

Wagner's music for his doomed pair is so powerful that it allows the audience to overlook their incestuous bond. But that bond is one of the principal complaints Fricka is able to adduce in her argument, which sets up the great dilemma of the second act. It begins as a conflict between genuine love and law (symbolized here by incest and the betrayal of Hunding). Yet it's important not to think of this as so easily weighted toward where the audience's sympathies lie. Wagner takes care to present Fricka with dignity here, not as a henpecking scold; on a certain level, the entire act can even be read as a projection of Wotan's inner psyche. Fricka serves as his superego; the law she defends lies at the basis of the god's claim to power. And herein the larger, central dilemma of the *Ring* gains clarity. To put it in terms external to the cycle, it is nothing less than the conflict between what we value above all else (best grasped by the idea of "love") and the compromises and limitations we are forced to impose on that value by the way the world really works (the "power" that is up for grabs now that the ring has been forged or, to recall *Tristan*, the "Will").

Der fliegende Holländer

Tannhäuser in the Venusberg

Lohengrin's arrival

Hans Sachs and the song contest in *Die Meistersinger*

San Francisco Opera: Larry Merkl

Tristan and Isolde

The Rhinedaughters and their gold with Alberich

Seattle Opera's "green"
Ring: Das Rheingold

Siegmund and Sieglinde

Wotan

Siegfried faces the dragon

Siegfried and Mime

Hagen and Alberich

Brünnhilde as Woman

Brünnhilde's Immolation

Parsifal and Gurnemanz

Amfortas

Erda's warning at the end of *Das Rheingold* gave Wotan his first inkling of how this dilemma will play out. But the focus there was still abstract. *Die Walküre* narrows the focus to present his point of view, sharpened now by the pain that he must undergo. The significance of his enormous monologue reverberates throughout the *Ring*. (The god himself describes his outburst as a monologue, even as he speaks to Brünnhilde, to whom he confides as if she were a part of himself.) Its effect is to make Wotan the cycle's true central character, supplanting the original hero Siegfried. Wagner clearly recognized this crux in *Die Walküre*. This is the *Ring*'s pivotal moment, as we witness Wotan consciously willing his own destruction: "Only one thing do I still desire: the End!"

Wotan suggests that these are thoughts that should remain unuttered. But the music's immediacy overrides the reluctance of his words: with its dark brooding passion, it tells listeners that they are again in the existential territory of the Flying Dutchman. One senses this in the spin on the motive of Wotan's Spear (symbol of his authority), which incorporates frustration in its new configuration. Much has been made of this as the philosophical turning point in the *Ring:* Wagner exchanging an earlier revolutionary optimism (inspired by Feuerbach's humanism) for the radical, quasi-Buddhist detachment from desire to which Schopenhauer's thought introduced him. Wagner himself often repeated his view that he had instinctively expressed the latter before finding it ratified in Schopenhauer. (The philosopher, for his part, seems not to have been impressed: Wagner's gift of a signed copy of the *Ring* texts met a cold silence in response.)

The most sensible way to approach these issues is to remain skeptical about any reductive tendencies—certainly with a work as ambitious and heterogeneous in its scope as the *Ring*. The truth is that it contains *all* these angles. But the *Ring* transcends any one philosophical orientation, just as it goes beyond issues of Wagner's artistic theories of the relative significance of music and words in the overall drama, and so on. One might even say that the *Ring* is about the futility of exactly such reductionism. The pattern pervading its universe is fraught with the negative effects of power, and every attempt to find a redeeming exception seems bound to fail. The "curse" motive is one musical shorthand for this pattern—and the one leitmotif that is arguably used too intrusively in the *Ring* (particularly in *Siegfried*). Yet the need to hope itself, most especially in the form of love, is just as integral to that universal pattern. The tension generated by this fundamental dilemma is so profoundly involving because it replicates the contradictions inherent in life. For Wagner, the *Ring* is concerned to show "how necessary it is to acknowledge change, variety, multiplicity and the eternal newness of reality and of life."

Brünnhilde illustrates this reality powerfully, particularly if one views events from her point of view: she faces the world from which Wotan has already decided to begin detaching himself. Indeed she at first mirrors his development, but she is out of phase with his own emotional state. The result is the great tragedy of the second half of *Die Walküre*. Young and full of hope, Brünnhilde first appears to a motive of elemental energy. This—and the attendant war cry, based on an augmented fifth chord—is of course the music threading through the *Ring*'s most famous excerpt, the "Ride of the Valkyries" opening act 3 (CD 2, track 4). Its introductory figurations in winds and strings (again, those "minimalist" repetitions) whip the trilling fire music of Loge into a frenzied storm (0:01); beneath this is added an impetuous dotted rhythm (0:08) against which the major-minor Valkyrie motive itself (0:21) strikes sparks.

As a backlash against its popularity, the "Ride of the Valkyries" has often been accused of relying on meretricious, cheap effects. But heard in context, the scene, with all its sardonic black humor, proves undeniably thrilling. As the voices enter with the Valkyrie war cry (1:18), we hear the first quasi-choral moments (3:58) of the *Ring* (apart from the Rhinemaidens' trio)—part of Wagner's attempts at a "surround-sound" acoustic effect. This is still in accord with Wagner's music drama principles, however, since the Valkyries are here perceived as essentially one character.

But as Wotan's favored daughter, Brünnhilde had already been differentiated from her sisters, and it becomes clear why in the remainder of the second act as the stories of the human lovers and of Wotan's dilemma intersect. Wagner feared that having these two titanic climaxes in the same act would strain endurance. Brünnhilde is present for both (Wotan's despairing confession and the death of Siegmund). She spends much of her time at first listening to her father. But this isn't a passive process, as her moving scene with Siegmund shows us. By listening to the doomed hero—that is, understanding his point of view and observing the depth of his love for Sieglinde—Brünnhilde learns what has eluded Wotan (the gods learning from humans is one of the *Ring*'s many potent ironies). Siegmund's refusal of the pleasures of Valhalla (to a beautiful musical depiction of false utopia, adorning the now-familiar theme with embroidery from harps and winds) teaches the Valkyrie the meaning of compassion that Sieglinde had introduced in the first act as she drew water for Siegmund.

Brünnhilde's moment of compassionate epiphany (to music that prefigures the "love glance" motive of *Tristan*) leads to her impulsive decision to defend Siegmund. Its fallout is the subject of the rest of the opera. Wotan's anger is so immense, terrifying even to the hardy Valkyries, because Brünnhilde has acted as he secretly desired. In other words, she acts out the hope he prefers not to admit—and, as he knew it must, the hope proved false, only confirming his sense of being trapped, of having no way out. Yet his daughter views the situation in a different light. This is the significance of her rescue of Sieglinde, now pregnant with the hero-to-be Siegfried (whom otherwise Wotan would destroy to avoid another sign of delusory hope). Sieglinde responds to the renewed lease on life Brünnhilde gives her with an ecstatic transport of melody; it will lie dormant until the *Ring*'s final scene, when Brünnhilde herself invokes it.

The final scene reverts to the chamberlike textures of the first act, as we move from the outer storm back to the realm of the psyche. In a beautiful turn of musical symbolism, Wagner manipulates Wotan's Spear motive into a stirring melody representing Brünnhilde's plea for mercy (CD 2, track 5, 2:21 ff), just as her action defies his pessimist determinism. Wotan eventually relents to soften his necessary punishment. The scoring intensifies into one of the great emotional climaxes of the entire cycle (3:27)—and one of its most complete moments of catharsis. Wotan's relationship with his daughter here offers possibly the only scene in all opera that can compare with *King Lear*.

Wotan's own education reaches a new stage through his loss, leaving Brünnhilde for the one who will be "freer than I, the god" (2:09). The motive of love's renunciation will later steal into the orchestra (7:04). This is a reminder of the ambivalence of the leitmotifs. For example, the assertive trumpet motive announcing Wotan's "great thought" at the end of *Das Rheingold* is finally associated with Siegmund's sword only in the first act of *Die Walküre*. But the leitmotifs can move in the opposite direction too, from concrete clarity to more complex associations. The first scene of *Das Rheingold* clearly links this motive with the renunciation of love. But it recurs portentously, obviously not to be taken "literally," when Siegmund prepares to draw the sword from the tree (he isn't renouncing love, but he is at a turning point as decisive as that when Alberich chooses the gold). We hear it now, as Wotan accepts his separation from his daughter. Its appearance causes us to reflect, while instinctively drawing our attention to the recurring tragedy of love at odds with the universal pattern of power.

Wagner follows with a wonderful symphonic development (8:54 ff) of Wotan's elegiac farewell melody (4:21). He interweaves it delicately with the hypnotic motive (8:44) of Brünnhilde's sleep (a variant of the Rhinemaidens' opening lullaby-like phrase). The opera closes with the celebrated "Magic Fire" music (starting with the commanding restatement of Wotan's Spear leitmotif at 10:54). More than any of the other gods who "disappear" into the orchestra following *Das Rheingold*, Loge will continue to play an extensive role, and this is one of his most glorious transformations (11:55). The roaring bravado ending the *Ring*'s "preliminary evening" is here replaced, after the final hopeful announcement of Siegfried's prophetic theme (12:56 ff), by a gentle, repetitive lull (14:18 ff). But its peacefulness resembles an uneasy whistling in the dark, serving to blunt the almost unbearable series of tragedies that have been witnessed.

Coming of Age
Siegfried

iegfried is, on one level, the *Ring*'s hidden comedy. Taken by itself, the opera pits its protagonist against a number of obstacles until he is successfully united with his beloved. Wagner's original title was *Der junge Siegfried;* he intended it to depict the hero as he comes of age, serving in his original scheme as a lighter, comic complement to the thoroughly tragic *Siegfried's Death* (that is, *Götterdämmerung*). *Siegfried,* for all its brooding, violent atmosphere, also comes closer to comedy in the more colloquial sense of the term than anyplace else in the *Ring* (save a few moments in *Das Rheingold*). It even includes what is possibly the *Ring*'s single one-liner: "Das ist kein Mann!" (That's not a man!), exclaimed by Siegfried as he loosens the breastplate from what he assumes is a male warrior, only to discover the sleeping Brünnhilde. A number of commentators have also likened *Siegfried* (presumably for both its playfulness and grotesqueries) to the scherzo within a gigantic metaphorical symphony spanned by the *Ring,* which is fun if you enjoy that sort of thing but basically a dead end.

The comic level, however, lies deeply buried beneath the weight of associations built up from the surrounding context of the *Ring*. On yet another level, *Siegfried* is actually two operas in one. Wagner's famous break from writing the *Ring* occurred between the second and third acts of *Siegfried*. This interval of a dozen years (spent in composing *Tristan* and *Die Meistersinger*) results in an unmistakable stylistic shift—an exciting part of experiencing the *Ring*—for the final act. Yet Wagner brilliantly fuses all these hybrid elements into a convincing whole: the sense of unity he creates, both within the opera and in terms of *Siegfried*'s relation to the rest of the *Ring,* is an achievement of breathtaking artistry.

Wagner forged ahead with *Siegfried* in September 1856 (having completed the scoring of *Die Walküre* in May). He was now entering his fourth year of intense musical focus on the *Ring.* By the following summer, however, artistic crisis loomed. Work on *Tristan* was beckoning, and prospects for seeing the *Ring* staged in any form remotely close to what Wagner intended seemed dimmer than ever. It's also likely that Wagner intuited the need for some distance to allow the *Ring* to mature even further within him. He had, after all, waited several years before undertaking *Das Rheingold;* quite possibly he didn't feel ready yet for the formidable task of setting the great encounters of the third act to music.

The composer may have sensed as well that he was approaching burnout on the *Ring.* While *Siegfried* offers among the loveliest and most thrilling moments in the cycle, the first two acts contain arguably some of its thinnest music as well. In June Wagner wrote to Liszt that he had left young Siegfried "beneath a linden tree" and was reluctantly confining him to his desk "under lock and key as though I were burying him alive." But he did wake him briefly, the next month, and completed his draft of the second act in August. Except for work on the final scoring of the first two acts between 1864 and 1865, *Siegfried* was then left to hibernate until the composer began work on the final act in March 1869, finishing the draft in June and its scoring in February 1871.

Siegfried is a hybrid not just stylistically but because of its innocent fairy-tale atmosphere, which is grafted onto the essentially tragic mythic structure of the entire *Ring*. Wagner had experimented with such genre fusion before (notably in *Lohengrin*). His enthusiasm in sensing a link between the Grimm Brothers' fairy tale about the boy who has not yet learned fear and the mythic saga was boundless: mostly because it seemed to corroborate Wagner's cherished idea of a core "poetic truth" contained within archetypal stories, whether in their mythic or fairy-tale variants. When the complete *Ring* was first staged in Bayreuth in 1876, the visual concept was basically limited to this storytelling aspect, with its dragon, winged helmets, and melancholy moonlit glens. The Metropolitan Opera's popular neoromantic and naturalistic production created in the 1980s by Otto Schenk and Gunther Schneider-Siemssen (and televised in 1990) revived much of this fairy-tale sensibility, albeit updated with state-of-the-art technology.

During the early stages of the *Ring*'s evolution, as Wagner was contemplating what path to take after *Lohengrin,* his imagination teemed with an array of possible subjects alongside the Nibelung myth. These included both historical and mythic figures. Wagner sketched out projected opera treatments of the emperor Frederick Barbarossa, a romantic fable called *Wieland der Schmied* (Wieland the Smith), the Homeric hero Achilles, and even Jesus (in an extraordinarily detailed scenario of his life and message called *Jesus of Nazareth;* written on the brink of the Dresden uprising, it projected a revolutionary social reformer whose love liberates humanity from a corrupt order). All of these were abandoned. Or rather, they became subsumed in and overshadowed by Wagner's original focal point for the *Ring:* the hero Siegfried, who represented a Rousseau-like exemplar of the "purely human," untainted by society (think of the famous salvo opening Rousseau's *The Social Contract:* "Man is born free; yet everywhere he is in chains"). A sense of the profound significance Wagner invested in him is clear from this description (in his letter to August Röckel of January 24, 1854): "In Siegfried I have tried to depict what I understand to be the most perfect human being."

It wasn't just Wagner who managed to load the mythic Siegfried with such a heavy freight. Shaw's *The Perfect Wagnerite* describes the young Siegfried as the archetype of the self-reliant "Protestant" and as an idealized anarchist, "a perfectly naïve hero upsetting religion, law and order in all directions and establishing in their place the unfettered action of Humanity doing exactly what it likes" (Shaw goes on to see this as a dramatization of the central idea in Adam Smith's *Wealth of Nations*). Friedrich Nietzsche, who was becoming friends with the composer just as he was writing the last act of *Siegfried* in 1869, developed ideas that resonate with more than a hint of this iconoclastic hero. The best known of these is Nietzsche's concept of the life-affirming *Übermensch* (superman) who must create his own value in the face of a meaningless universe.

Despite the role of comedy in conceiving Siegfried, one of Wagner's most telling comments on the *Ring* as a whole concerns the psychology of fear (again, from his January 1854 letter to Röckel): "We must learn to die, and to die in the fullest sense of the word; fear of the end is the source of all lovelessness, and this fear is generated only when love itself is already beginning to wane." Fear, in this deeper sense, arises from a reluctance to accept change—change being the underlying reality of the world, according to Wagner elsewhere in the same letter. As a motivating force, fear is then akin to greed for power as a foil to love's redeeming role. Siegfried acquires special significance as "a fearless human being, one who never ceases to love."

The interplay of fear and foreboding certainly has a revelatory, even dominating, role in the *Ring*. From the moment that Alberich steals the gold, fear recurs as an emotional leitmotif. It ripples through *Das Rheingold* in the fear that the subjugated Nibelungs feel for Alberich and that he himself faces when he loses the ring. Anxiety, furthermore, pervades the opera's final scene, despite its pseudotriumphal conclusion. This sense of insecurity then reaches tragic heights in its effects on Wotan in *Die Walküre*.

And fear takes center stage from the moment *Siegfried* begins, in counterpoint to its humor. One hears it in the brooding depths of the prelude. The music sounds out Mime's point of view as he seems to intermingle memories of his tortured past with dreams of gaining control of the Nibelung hoard himself. The grotesque and shadowy scoring for bassoons, timpani, and violas against plucked strings echoes the scherzo of Beethoven's Fifth Symphony even more obviously than the somber pianissimos mentioned in regard to *Die Walküre*. This fear as a motivating force dominates the action of *Siegfried* both negatively and positively. For Mime and Alberich, fear is allied with the humiliation and powerlessness that intensifies their longing for the ring. Wotan's appearances to both dwarves on the other hand represent a reversal: he seems to have overcome his own fear and thus lost interest in the ring. And indeed his new persona as the "Wanderer" has frequent comic overtones, particularly in the riddle game of wits he plays with Mime.

But for young Siegfried, the absence of fear acts as a spur to acquire experience. His very eagerness "to learn" fear—fear in this sense as a challenge to face change—leads him first to slay the dragon and ultimately to find Brünnhilde. This double-sidedness of fear is apparent from the start: comically, with the stage business about the bear Siegfried brings in to frighten Mime, but more broadly in the exaggerated contrasts between the dwarf and his foster son. *Wagner's Ring and Its Symbols,* Robert Donington's study, draws on Jungian psychology to explore the entire cycle as a marvelous inward journey, an epic of the human psyche in its quest for maturity and integration of the self. Donington believes Mime's "double dose of fear" represents the idea that he "carries the part of Siegfried's shadow which holds his fear, his meanness and in short the unheroic side of him." Siegfried hates Mime in a classic projection: "If Mime did not stand for unconscious attributes of Siegfried's own, Siegfried would not hate him; he would merely be indifferent."

Donington views Siegfried's "strange upbringing" as a prototype for the "emergence from animal consciousness into human consciousness." Unfortunately, the emphasis on the primitive here results in a portrait of the hero as a young brute. Nowhere else in Wagner's entire work is the disparity between his lofty ideals of a character and his actual dramatization so painfully apparent. For many *Ring* aficionados, Siegfried comes off in the first act as little more than a swaggering bully, stupid and callous rather than "uncorrupted." He's a cousin to the wolf child whom we will see again, but in a much subtler light, in the figure of Parsifal. The musical analog to this rawness is the main motive associated with young Siegfried, his horn call.

In contrast to the prophetically resonant Siegfried theme announced at the end of *Die Walküre* (which will gain prominence as the opera progresses), this naïve and energetic motto, especially in the resonant horn register, echoes the natural world of harmony depicted in *Das Rheingold.* Its simplicity reminds listeners that the cycle will continue as a sort of Bildungsroman of Siegfried maturing into the "man of the future" who was part of Wagner's original vision for the *Ring.* On one level, the rest of the *Ring* cycle is about the transformations that occur relevant to this motive. They become a microcosm for the larger tragedy of how the nature-born Siegfried confronts and in turn is shaped by the world outside him.

Siegfried's intensifying curiosity about his origins shapes the first act and recapitulates the *Ring*'s own quest for origins (exemplified by the "beginning" depicted in *Das Rheingold*'s prelude). The prominence of closed song-forms here is hardly coincidental. Such balladlike elements as Mime's lament and Siegfried's "Forging Song" (CD 2, track 6) betray a ritualistic quality in their repetitions. It is as if these heightened moments of song are part of the story that has been retold countless times during Siegfried's upbringing. The raw power of his heroic octave-stretches as he calls the sword's name (0:01) echoes his father Siegmund's music before pulling the Notung from the tree in the first act of *Die Walküre*. Both moments suggest the desperate last-minute summoning of energy needed finally to break free: in Siegfried's case, from the falsely lulling repetitions of his foster parent Mime, a break that is essential for the hero to move on to the next stage. The impressive, fate-portending bass line (0:49) is clearly meant to evoke the descending line of Wotan's Spear and all the compromises it stands for. But above this, Siegfried's heroic tone exudes a will forceful enough to suggest a way out of the larger world of limitations this too implies. Accompanying it is another beautiful variation on the fire music (the upper registers starting at 3:16, for example); for Siegfried, like Wotan before him, will subdue the power of Loge to his own needs in forging the sword anew. This passage subliminally implants a connection that becomes crystal clear as he succeeds. Siegmund's sword had been absorbed into the tragic pattern traced by the *Ring* as Wotan's Spear shattered it, as well as the freeing hope it represented. Siegfried's forging restores that hope, even pointing toward a possible way out of the pattern.

That pattern arises from the nature of power. But the cal-culating cruelty that subjugates others and the fear that moti-vates preemptive strategies are not the only varieties of power explored in the *Ring.* Just as central is the power of nature, the force that after all serves as the musical germ cell at the begin-ning of the cycle. Nature entails a profound ambivalence. We hear this in the inertia and shadows of the act 2 prelude, with its unstable tritone harmonies. Nature, after all, shows many faces in the *Ring.* Even its primal innocence is ambiguous, as recalled from the Rhinemaidens' teasing, which set the entire plot in motion. Nature in the form of the storms of *Die Walküre* bears a threatening aspect and is an analog for psychic unrest. And nature is deeply allied with the role of the unconscious: the sleep into which Brünnhilde sinks, the sleep for which Erda longs, or the brooding, inchoate sound world of the dark cave in which Fafner sleeps in a kind of psychic hibernation.

Yet nature plays a redemptive role as the life force that is intimately linked to love. Wagner displays this link musi-cally again and again, repeating it with particular emphasis in a scene called the "Forest Murmurs" (track 7): the peaceful oasis in act 2 in which Siegfried, left to himself, is observed to muse about his dead mother and to commune with nature. It is the analog to the brief oasis of love in act 1 of *Die Walküre,* as profound in its resonance—and as transient. Before Siegfried has learned fear or human love (the two will be interlaced in the opera's final act), he enjoys a transfiguring moment in the forest. A rapturous passage in the strings (0:29 ff) derives from the music originally heard in connection with Freia and her golden apples. Wavy oscillations shimmer (0:56); their rustlings evoke those protominimalist passages (above all asso-ciated with water) from *Das Rheingold,* while against birdsong in the flute and oboe a foregrounded melody from the clarinet (1:14), soon to be associated with the Woodbird, is sister to the

Rhinemaidens' opening lullaby. The ethereal fabric of sound in the "Forest Murmurs" creates a sense of heightened conscious-ness, of Siegfried finding himself at one with the universe.

Wagner's concept of young Siegfried has much in common with the "holy fool" that was a treasured *idée fixe* in nineteenth-century literature. It will figure even more forcefully in *Parsifal.* But Siegfried's spontaneous contact with nature also brings to mind a celebrated essay by Friedrich Schiller that, in our own time, has inspired the composer John Adams to write an orchestral work with the same title. *Über naïve und sentimen-talische Dichtung* (On Naïve and Reflective Poetry) must rank among the top ten greatest pieces of art criticism ever written. Briefly, Schiller distinguishes between two archetypes among creative personalities. The "naïve" feels at one with nature and is on the objective, spontaneous, classical end of the spectrum (Homer, Shakespeare, Goethe, and Mozart are exemplars). The "reflective" or "sentimental" is the subjective, romantic creator who is alienated from nature, the self-conscious and tormented artist (think Tchaikovsky, Eugene O'Neill, or to a large extent, Wagner himself). Schiller's masterful essay isn't remotely so schematic, but for our purposes, these can be seen as polar categories to which the characters in the *Ring* (and in all of Wagner's works) belong. Wotan is the "sentimental" figure par excellence, while Siegfried is at his most "naïve" in the "Forest Murmurs" scene. His unselfconscious enjoyment of natural beauty recalls a lost innocence, but more importantly, it prefigures a possible new utopia. And it points toward that transfiguring moment of redemption *within* nature that *Parsifal*'s "Good Friday Spell" enacts (CD 1, track 10).

But this scene is an oasis, if not a mirage, in the *Ring*'s dan-gerous world. On either side yawn very dark elements indeed. Preceding it, Alberich's appearance marks the first time we have seen him (he had retreated into the score in *Die Walküre*) since he pronounced his curse on the ring. Now he reminds the audience of what is at stake with the ring still at large in the world. His presence here ranges from pure malice (an intensification, really, of his fear in *not* having the ring) to the laughable pettiness of the tantrum he throws in the altercation with his brother Mime. On the other side, Fafner as dragon underscores the ambiguous power of nature once again. Inevitably, the actual appearance of Fafner in visible form tends to be a disappointment: the vividness of Wagner's music is far more frightening than a papier-mache, mammoth-jawed beast could ever be (and has become one of the more interesting challenges for production designers). And this part of the second act contains moments of unadulterated ugliness that glaringly contrast with the beauty of the "Forest Murmurs" scene.

Siegfried's comic aspects abound particularly in how the Mime-Siegfried relationship is depicted. Wagner resorts to much black humor, as in the dwarf's ravings while Siegfried continues with his forging (e.g., track 6, 2:47). With Fafner now dead, Mime sets about his plan. The exchange in which Siegfried acquires the ability to "hear" Mime's real intentions after tasting the dragon's blood is a tour de force: the dwarf protests with increasing frustration, unaware that his mask of flattering lies is useless before Siegfried's new X-ray perception. It even operates as a metaphor for Wagner's music drama, drawing attention to the ever-present issue of whence the meaning arises: from the orchestra or from the words? Can one be lulled away—rather than guided—by the music into a state of inattention to the true significance unfolding (as Mime attempts to charm Siegfried with his melodic line)?

It's a fascinating interlude, which brings out the hidden comedy within *Siegfried*. But Mime's chilling murder introduces a profoundly unsettling rupture. The parody and caricature that go into Mime actually create a memorable character. For all his treachery, his plans for the power that was supposed to come his way with the ring were not nearly so menacing as Alberich's. Rather like that of Smeagol/Gollum in *The Lord of the Rings*, his strong characterization induces a sympathy in the light of which Siegfried's act makes him loathsome, despite the argument of self-defense; one is reluctant to see Mime written out of the cycle.

Ironically, the killing of Mime is the turning point that leads Siegfried to lose his "naïve" peace of mind for a moment and to face his loneliness. This loneliness is the first step on his way from innocence to experience: to face fear and ultimately love. It's a counterpart to the narcissistic images of water and reflections described by the hero earlier as he searched for his identity. The music of act 3 will provide an unforgettable description of this condition of loneliness and contrast it with the next stage in Siegfried's development.

The striking shift that happens musically in act 3 is instantly noticeable to the ear but virtually impossible to describe. One angle that's typically used to explain this shift is to recall that by this point, Wagner had composed both *Tristan* and *Die Meistersinger*. And indeed the influence of both is profound hereafter in the *Ring* cycle. It has to do with a more comprehensively symphonic imagination: the intricate, even aggressive counterpoint in which leitmotifs are now interwoven forms a richer fabric. There's also a pliant, suppler use of the orchestra and an even more refined gradation of instrumental colors and shading effects.

It is somehow fitting that the character to whom this mature stylistic sense is first applied is Wotan, for his character arguably undergoes the most extensive development within the *Ring* (Brünnhilde is also a contender for that claim). Ironically, as Wagner's cycle evolved, Wotan had usurped the central role initially reserved for Siegfried. The churning, anxious prelude to act 3 gives the audience entrée into this new corner of the *Ring*'s universe. It links motives from *Das Rheingold* with the wide-ranging harmonic sequence of chords representing Wotan's guise as the Wanderer—the moniker by which he is known throughout *Siegfried*. Wotan's transformation into the mysterious stranger, cloaked in blue and professing a newfound detachment from the problems that beset him in the first two operas of the *Ring,* adds a wonderful dimension to his character. His interactions with Mime (in the folkloric riddle contest of act 1) and with Alberich suggest the wisdom he has gained from his firsthand suffering in *Die Walküre*. He even refers philosophically to the interconnection between himself and the Nibelung: "Licht Alberich" vs. "Schwarz Alberich."

Although changed from the proud and arrogant lord of Valhalla to the aloof Wanderer, Wotan has little in common with the Dutchman and other Wagnerian wanderers until this final act, which is also his final bow from the *Ring*'s stage. Here we get flashes of his earlier intensity, which the composer's recharged musical style evokes magnificently in the encounter with Erda and then with Siegfried. Wotan's burning desire to learn the ultimate questions from Erda parallels the hero's desire to learn in the opera: about his origins, about fear, about love. And Wotan's own fear seems to rekindle as he reveals that he in fact has not yet completely escaped the pattern so tragically dramatized in *Die Walküre*: he still holds a pocket of hope that the world (his world) can be set right.

Wagner's skills as a dramatist are at their peak here as he prepares for the encounter with Siegfried: it has the mythical-tragic force of Sophocles' Oedipus. This scene is one of the *Ring*'s great cruxes, where the human and divine planes meet up and face each other. For once the hero's pushy impetuosity wins us over as he stands opposite the powerful force of Wotan. This is the moment in which Wagner's split self-portraits in the *Ring*—and all they represent of his philosophy, his shifting world view, his musical evolution—stare each other down.

Wotan/the Wanderer, however, is not prepared to go gently into that good night. Those who pursue the psychological acuity of Wagner's operas turn to this encounter as a high point of proto-Freudian insight. Siegfried's defiance causes Wotan's memories of his own past dreams to flare up, while the (grand)son undertakes the deed of metaphorically slaying the patriarch. The paired, interconnected musical processes of fragmentation and integration operate throughout the *Ring* as a musical equivalent to the same psychic processes within the characters. Both are heard in close proximity here. As Siegfried splits Wotan's Spear, its motive shatters (painfully, in contrast to the beautiful reshaping of it Brünnhilde accomplishes at the end of *Die Walküre*): Wotan accepts the inevitable. Then, after a series of powerful silences, the musical temperature rises for the ascent of the Magic Mountain surrounded by fire. The brief tone poem (corresponding to the scene change) involves a grand integration of Siegfried's simple horn call with his more mature prophetic theme, all set against a dazzling orchestration of the fire music.

Extraordinarily colorful as this synthesis is, it represents only one part of the process of Siegfried's maturing. The noisily extroverted music of the fire-crossing is followed by a searing, quasi-atonal line in the violins, which meanders and ascends to a piercing altitude. The effect is to bring together Siegfried's daring and the loneliness glimpsed at the end of act 2: his passage, one senses, is both outer and inner at the same time, a confrontation with his own psyche. The marvelous final scene of the opera brings all this to the fore. Siegfried, after all, does learn fear: but he learns it by awakening Brünnhilde, by awakening his own dormant sexual desire—for desire, as is now clear in the world of the *Ring,* is ineluctably connected with the possibility of loss, with the fundamental reality of change. But by presenting fear in this context, it's as if Wagner is suggesting a way for love to redeem fear.

The music of Brünnhilde's awakening is of an overwhelm-ing beauty. This, more than any, is the music Wagner must have needed to wait for, as Brünnhilde awaited her waker, to ripen in the long period he spent away from the *Ring*. It's a musical passage that conveys transformation, the coming to a new level of consciousness; and it will return in a pivotal moment of *Götterdämmerung* (track 10, 3:13 ff). The music is highly ecstatic, solemn and blazing with joy at the same time. Donington's archetypal readings of symbols in the *Ring* seem especially apropos here. They have a stage analog in the now-legendary postwar productions of Wieland Wagner that were introduced in Bayreuth in 1951. On one level, their intent was to cleanse associations with the ugly Nazi past by erasing tradi-tional stagings and starting with a tabula rasa. But the central idea, with the two lovers on a simple revolving disc and evoca-tive lighting patterns, highlighted the abstract, timeless world of archetype and myth.

The final twenty minutes of the opera present the fluctuating emotions of this mutual awakening of Siegfried and Brünnhilde: he to the reality and ecstasy of human love, she to her loss of divinity but newly gained humanity. A new set of themes unre-lated to the network of leitmotifs that have developed all along is suddenly introduced (Wagner extracted these for the lovely chamber orchestra piece he wrote on the occasion of Cosima's birthday in 1870, the so-called *Siegfried Idyll*). There's a power-ful opulence to the love music that contrasts intriguingly with *Tristan,* considering that here the lovers sing the praises of sun and the light (negating the values of "night" in *Tristan*). In the climactic minutes of the love duet (track 8), Wagner relaxes his theoretical rules to the most striking extent thus far in the

Ring as the pair not only overlap but intermingle their vocal lines (4:51).

An essential part of Siegfried's education is to overcome his aloneness: Wagner had written long before composing this music that "not even Siegfried alone (man alone) is the complete 'human being': he is merely the half, only with Brünnhilde does he become the redeemer...for it is love which is really 'the eternal feminine' itself." The braiding together of the lovers' vocal lines beautifully symbolizes this yin and yang aspect of the pair. But the love music and its lyrics have a strange qual- ity: both defiant and ecstatic at the same time, full of manic energy. It contains robust, mock-folk-music lines (4:20) and even a traditional ringing high C (5:40), the latter reminding listeners of the sunny, extroverted home key of *Die Meistersinger.* What the two sing, however—"gleaming love, laughing death" (5:17)—suggests an attitude clearly inhabiting a different world from that of Eva, Walther, or Sachs. The meaning of this love will become pivotal in the unfolding of the *Ring's* finale, *Götterdämmerung.*

In the End Is the Beginning

Götterdämmerung

Whatever form they take—romantically naturalistic, Freudian, Shavian socialist allegory, or even postmodern sci-fi—productions of the *Ring* tend to foreground the central conflict as that between power and love. Yet underlying this polarity is an even more fundamental phenomenon: the reality of change and flux, as Wagner himself characterized it. *Götterdämmerung* is the epitome of change in two key senses. Its drama is dominated by a series of stark reversals of fortune. Moreover, it embodies at its core Wagner's original concept for the *Ring* cycle; like an archeological dig, *Götterdämmerung* contains several layers that betray the changes in Wagner's shifting philosophical, political, and aesthetic positions. Aspects of old-fashioned grand opera coexist with the revolutionary principles of music drama, corresponding to the different stages in Wagner's artistic evolution that become expressed in the *Ring* cycle.

Even the title *Götterdämmerung* encodes the *Ring*'s basic transfer of emphasis. The whole idea began with the drama Wagner called *Siegfrieds Tod*. After his expansion into four operas to tell the story, he changed the title to *Götterdämmerung*—the most abstract title of the four operas. This change neatly encapsulates the seismic conceptual shift from Siegfried (liberating, revolutionary hero) to Wotan (Will-renouncing pessimist) as the pivotal character in the *Ring*. The most widely used translation is (markedly with no definite article) *Twilight of the Gods*. But in *The Perfect Wagnerite,* Shaw offers the intriguing alternatives *Night Falls on the Gods* and *Godsgloaming*. The latter, incidentally, gives a marvelous taste of the quality of the German that Wagner devised for his verse throughout the *Ring*. Its mixture of heavy alliteration and neologisms to emphasize word roots results in a pseudo-archaic aura. It sounds just as weird to Germans as *gloaming* does to a native English speaker of the twenty-first century.

Shaw was well aware of the changes affecting *Götter-dämmerung*. Instead of a fascinating archeological dig, to him they represent mere relics of a tired past, an anticlimax to the *Ring*. For Shaw, what had begun as a revealing and profound allegory ends up as the gesture of a disillusioned, aging artist who had given up on his ideals. He views this finale to the *Ring* as a sort of victim of the strange reverse chronology of its creation: *Götterdämmerung*'s drama reverts back to Wagner's prerevolutionary period and is basically nothing but grand old opera. By the time he turned to composing it, Wagner had succumbed to a desire to "Lohengrinize" once more, as Shaw puts it. His interpretation is a lucid example of how the *Ring* functions as a kind of mirror to those who probe its meanings. *The Perfect Wagnerite* contains a swarm of insights that are still compelling. But since his own theory begins to fall apart pretty much where he feels the socialist allegory collapses (at the beginning of act 3 of *Siegfried*), Shaw inevitably gives the rest of the cycle short shrift. In a nutshell, although at the very highest and most entertaining level, Shaw replicates the myopia that one sees over and over with reductionist attempts to interpret Wagner.

Despite the changes encapsulated in *Götterdämmerung,* Wagner's achievement in completing his cycle can scarcely be overestimated. It was impressive enough to pick up after a break of a dozen tumultuous years and finish an incomplete opera. But *Siegfried* represents a smaller-scale version of what Wagner faced with *Götterdämmerung*. This was a dramatic idea he had conceived at thirty-five and had begun composing at forty. Now approaching his sixties, Wagner had to imagine the musical climax of his arduous journey with the *Ring* and to carry it off convincingly. And for all the cycle's internal contradictions and unresolved issues, it's difficult not to be awed by the underlying unity that holds all the pieces together. This is not a mechanical unity, a paint-by-numbers totality, but a deeply coherent, intricately woven fabric of connections that reinforce each other: an aesthetic unity as counterweight to the very multiplicity and change at the heart of the *Ring*'s universe.

Wagner began composing *Götterdämmerung* in the fall of 1869—shortly after the birth of his first son, whom he named, unsurprisingly, Siegfried (his desire was for Siegfried to avoid music and become a surgeon, but his son did in fact follow in father's footsteps as an opera composer). The following year he was finally able to marry Cosima. The emotional security Wagner enjoyed during this period may have contributed to the sense of consolidation that permeates *Götterdämmerung*. Yet the composer's woes were far from over. He had recently been humiliated by being forced to allow the premature world premieres of *Das Rheingold* and *Die Walküre,* per King Ludwig's orders, in Munich. Meanwhile, the financial backing essential for building his new Bayreuth Festival Theater continued to prove elusive, even after Wagner had laid the foundation stone in 1872 (on May 22, his birthday) and resettled with his family in the Bayreuth villa he named "Wahnfried" (Illusion's Peace). Thus it's not surprising that composition of *Götterdämmerung* was beset by numerous delays. Perhaps Wagner also experienced a certain reluctance to finish the cycle that had consumed such a vast part of his creative life: the inevitable anticlimax rather than relief of drawing to a conclusion. He eventually committed the final chord to paper in his full score on November 21, 1874. *Götterdämmerung* would reach the stage as the finale of the world's first *Ring Cycle* presented at Bayreuth in August 1876—twenty-eight years after Wagner had conceived this first version of *Götterdämmerung*.

The lengthy prelude is an unusual feature within the *Ring*'s dramaturgy. The other three operas all begin *in medias res* (even *Das Rheingold,* after depicting "the beginning"). *Götterdämmerung*'s stylized scene with the Norns is one of those layers from the work's earliest stage. Their narration of the back story was what originally led Wagner to realize that more was needed: that is, rather than mere exposition, dramatic presentation on a larger scale was the only way to achieve the desired resonance. This need wasn't only dramatic but musical as well. In fact, the earliest sketches for the *Ring*'s music date from 1850 and are precisely for this scene. This was apparently the point when Wagner stepped back and decided to unfold the story in a series of operas: "It will all imprint itself graphically by means of sharply defined physical images, it will all be understood—so that by the time they hear the more serious 'Siegfried's Death,' the audience will know all the things that are taken for granted or simply hinted at there."

So why didn't Wagner then cut this narrative scene—not to mention parallel ones in *Götterdämmerung* and elsewhere in the *Ring?* A less-than-satisfying answer is that some of the information imparted is new, adding details to the action that has already been presented. But the issue is more complex than it might at first seem. Carl Dahlhaus astutely pinpoints what is involved in his overview in the 1980 *New Grove Wagner*. He suggests that Wagner's original attempt to set the scene in 1850 failed because the background he was attempting to convey was still too abstract and therefore "musically colorless and thin." The decision to expand the story into four operas therefore arose "not only from dramatic but also musical reasons": which is to say, the music needed space for the motives to be intro-duced properly and then to register in the audience.

The crucial paradox, Dahlhaus explains, is between the *Ring*'s dramatic and epic (that is, narrative or reflective) ele-ments. Originally, the Norns were providing mere narrative exposition; now that the preceding dramas have unfolded, their function is one of recapitulation, of taking stock in a new context. The gains afforded by the dramatic expansion don't obviate the need for the epic elements but in fact enhance them: "far from shrinking, they grew," Dahlhaus observes. This is because "epic recapitulation of what has already been shown visually actually creates opportunities for passages particularly rich in motivic development. The epic traits that Wagner the dramatist mistrusted were restored out of musical necessity."

Another way of thinking of this process is to recall the musical function of the recapitulation in a symphony's sonata movements. Although we hear the repetition of musical mate-rial, it should sound transformed and renewed by what has intervened. These reflective, epic moments in the final part of the *Ring* indeed have a highly symphonic quality—most obvi-ously of course when the score itself involves a purely instru-mental interlude, such as in Siegfried's "Rhine Journey" and the Funeral March, but also in narrative scenes of retrospect: the Norns, Waltraute's plea, Siegfried's exploits re-enacted through memory, and Brünnhilde's climactic scene.

In a good production, the prelude with the Norns introduces a dream world that exists outside the time zone—with all its overflowing human passions—of the opera to come. It forms a kind of pocket outside them, reminding us of the cosmological dimension behind these events, rather like the musical prelude to *Das Rheingold*. Although hinting of the trio of *Macbeth*'s witches, the Norns are not malevolent: if anything, considering they are the all-knowing spinners of fate, they're remarkably passive, pallid creatures, notably less differentiated than the three Rhinemaidens. Their presence emphasizes the *Ring*'s depiction of fate as the working of the unconscious, the region where, as Donington describes it, "the dark and the light sides of the psyche must confront each other." For him, this inner psychic journey is where the entire *Ring* has led: "[I]t is with effecting the necessary reconciliation between them that the remainder of the drama will be concerned."

Musically, Wagner's late style is perfectly suited to imbuing this scene with character—just what was missing, one surmises, in that first go back in 1850. The dreary Norns may be only telling the audience, but the score *shows* much. The opera begins with the chord progression (albeit transposed) heard at Brünnhilde's awakening in act 3 of *Siegfried*. Here Wagner links it to an elaboration of the nature music from the beginning of *Das Rheingold*. This never gives a sense of mere repetition. The symphonic intricacy and ripe orchestration of Wagner's late style create a profoundly suggestive sound world. He gives musical ideas now richly associated with beginning and renewal another spin by juxtaposing them with a language of increased harmonic ambiguity and wan colors from muted strings. Even Loge, who once prided himself on not having to eat Freia's golden apples to maintain his youth, now sounds decrepit in the transformation of his signature music. The result is an uncanny atmosphere that amplifies the oracular tone of the Norns; they seem on the verge of awareness that the world order must shed its skin to make way for something new. Their sudden agitation in the tearing of the rope of fate quickens the tension that has slowly been building through the scene. This tension suggests the rift between the passive fatalism of the *Ring*'s cosmology and

Wagner's original, optimistic attitude that there is a redemptive way outside the world's pattern symbolized by the ring
and its curse.

Wagner described his musical technique as the "art of transition" with reference to *Tristan,* achieving a shift in dramatic
temperature so subtly that it passes beneath conscious awareness. But he puts this art to masterful use in *Götterdämmerung,*
particularly in the transition to the second part of the prelude.
The melancholy edge of night has subtly shifted to dawn, while
the Norns' cosmic frettings give way to the hope-filled, human
joy of new lovers. Siegfried and Brünnhilde appear as they were
left at the end of the previous opera. Musically, however, one
is aware of the transformations each has undergone. Two new
motives associated with them throughout *Götterdämmerung*
appear first in the orchestra during this transition music.
Siegfried's is actually a metamorphosis of his naïve horn tune
into a maturely "heroic" mold suggested by full brass harmoni-
zation and an arresting shift in rhythmic emphasis. Brünnhilde
meanwhile retains her association with the energetic Valkyrie
motive but is now further characterized by one of the *Ring*'s
loveliest leitmotifs. Starting with an Italianate turn, its widespread intervals echo both the rising sixth and the love theme
that earlier characterized Siegmund and Sieglinde. This motive
portrays Brünnhilde's ecstatic acceptance of her woman-
hood, which she has gained from Siegfried at the price of her
divinity.

The pair's final love scene in *Siegfried* contained echoes of
Tristan's chromaticism. But here, as the duet proceeds to a
climax, the sexual passion binding them is unmistakable—
a remnant perhaps of Wagner's pre-Schopenauerian views of
sex as a path to wisdom and fullness. It's worth noting too that
this moment, crowned by the lovers joining voices in a jubilant
third (with Brünnhilde's ringing high C on top) represents the

last oasis of love in the *Ring*. As seen, love has repeatedly proved fleeting, with little staying power. The overjoyed triumph of love experienced by Siegfried and Brünnhilde may sound inde-structible, but it will be subjected to the same pattern and sur-vive only as an echo to be invoked—to tragic consequences.

Hereafter, following Siegfried's symphonic journey down the Rhine to the court of the Gibichungs and the beginning of the tragedy proper, the rest of the *Ring* remains unremittingly dark. It's fascinating to listen to the musical alchemy of late Wagner. Musical material that is by now highly familiar and full of associations becomes twisted and stretched into sonorities of an often frightening, profoundly unsettling magnificence. Shaw's complaints about the old-fashioned "Lohengrinizing" seem petty here, for Wagner galvanizes the staid conventions of grand opera with a dark tonal and harmonic palette that serves as one of opera's most probing depictions of evil. Take the ultra-simple semitone descent signifying despair (originally uttered by Alberich at the beginning of *Das Rheingold* as the motive of lament). Wagner freights it now with crushing, threatening chords to depict the alienation of the half-human Hagen. In his oversize ambition, Hagen figures as a villain even more powerful than his father Alberich. Another example of *Götterdämmerung*'s peculiarly crepuscular sound world is the sudden prominence of the uncanny Tarnhelm motive. It was spooky enough when first introduced as one of the first talismans of Alberich's new power in *Das Rheingold;* here it returns, practically a character in its own right, a central plot device as well as symbol for the transformations undergone by Siegfried. Wagner's harmonies are even richer now in their ambiguity, pointing the way toward the language of *Parsifal*.

Far from the pivotal, redeeming character Wagner once envisioned, Siegfried proves to be the weak link in the *Ring*'s final opera. After all the set-up for his development and emergence as a hero, he's really no more than a puppet readily manipulated by the first pathetic instances of civilized society he chances upon. The magic potion that erases his memory causes him to live only in the present moment and inflames his sexual passion for the first woman he sees, Gutrune. Siegfried's brutal ploy to capture Brünnhilde only emphasizes the crudity of his character. But it provides a fascinating musico-dramatic counterpart to the dichotomy of appearance and reality seen in Mime's feigning right before his slaying in act 2 of *Siegfried.*

Rather than the education of Siegfried, the focus of *Götterdämmerung* seems to shift to the education of Brünnhilde. Soprano Jane Eaglen, one of the leading exponents of the role today, has observed how her character evolves through the cycle: "You can hear her development in the way Wagner writes for her voice. The *Siegfried* Brünnhilde, for example, has a much higher tessitura than the *Walküre* Brünnhilde. It sounds more womanly." And within *Götterdämmerung* itself, there seem to be three different Brünnhildes: the new woman who has discovered love, the victim of a vicious betrayal who turns to vengeance, and the enlightened visionary (in each act, respectively).

Her scene with Waltraute develops the "womanly" figure seen in the prelude. Brünnhilde, who once observed the love between Siegfried's parents and learned from it, is now herself an eloquent advocate of that love. The confrontation with her Valkyrie sister is a brilliant touch. First, it's an example of the epic space described above, which allows the associated musical motives to unfold in new combinations and recapitulations. Even more, it pits the epic directly against the dramatic: Waltraute is an emissary from the epic past—and the only representative of the gods actually *seen* in *Götterdämmerung.* She represents the old world, the old order that Brünnhilde is now happy to see fall away. She is, as it were, the Old World to Brünnhilde's New World of love discovered. Tellingly, the visual correlative of this scene is the ring. Throughout the cycle, it has been a negative presence: possession of the ring entails bringing on its curse. Brünnhilde enacts a sudden reversal. The ring becomes a positive value as a symbol not of power but of love. Her dramatic reality, in other words, serves as a foil to the epic inevitability of the *Ring*.

Yet part of Brünnhilde's complexity in *Götterdämmerung* is that she straddles both worlds until she finally can bridge the rift between them. The trauma she must undergo involves some of the most violent passions represented in the entire cycle. At the end of act 1, when Siegfried in disguise overpowers her, Brünnhilde is all too ready to revert to the old way of thinking represented by Waltraute: to believe her love was just an illusion and that the pattern of disappointment and betrayal is indeed the pattern of the world. Her education will be to see beyond this.

Hagen meanwhile is the focal point of the darkness in *Götterdämmerung*. Wagner uses extensive musical parody and satire to depict a number of his creepy characters: Mime, Beckmesser in *Die Meistersinger,* even Alberich in his earliest appearance. Hagen is absolutely humorless and returns us to the kind of unremitting evil Wagner hadn't characterized since Ortrud in *Lohengrin*. His character is painted with chilling effect in the opening of the second act, in the scene known as "Hagen's Watch" (CD 2, track 9). In part a demonic rewrite of the apparition of the ghost in *Hamlet,* Alberich appears in a semi–dream state to his sleeping son, forcing him to swear that he will avenge him by obtaining the ring. Wagner sets himself a musical challenge here: to differentiate the kinds of evil of these two closely related characters. The orchestral fabric is eerie and hallucinatory, making much use of veiled colors and off-center rhythms (0:05). Instead of the fierce and forceful

music Hagen uses in his public appearances (his blaring cow
horn is a counterpart to Siegfried's horn call and is related to
Hunding's brutish clan calls sounded at the end of act 2 in *Die
Walküre*), the music here is curiously understated—it looks
ahead to the impressionism of Debussy (1:48). Wagner implies
the resoluteness of Hagen (1:18) in contrast to his father's
anxious impotence (2:12). It's a distinction between different
species of hatreds. The scene's misty half-light dissolves into
dawn, repeating the transition from the act 1 prelude, as Hagen
immediately sets about his goal of entrapping Siegfried. He is,
unlike Hamlet, a man of resolute action, to counterbalance
Siegfried's heroic decisiveness.

This swiftly paced second act is certainly the most
"Lohengrinized" aspect of *Götterdämmerung,* centered as it
is around an interrupted and fateful wedding celebration.
Formally, this is the point most replete with breaches of *Opera
and Drama* decorum. Wagner gives his audience not only several
full choruses but dramatic ensembles of characters and even an
old-fashioned revenge trio. In place of the clarifying simplicity
of the two-character scenes that dominate so much of the *Ring,*
this is indeed the social world of *Lohengrin.* And *Lohengrin* was,
after all, the opera Wagner had written prior to creating the
libretto for the drama at the center of *Götterdämmerung.* The
trio's incantation of the phrase "Siegfried's death" recalls the
original work from which the *Ring* would later grow. But note
that this isn't merely a musical throwback—Wagner's potent
harmonic language and continual use of leitmotifs are incorporated into the texture. In a sense, just as the musical fabric of
the *Ring* becomes progressively more polyphonic (particularly
in *Götterdämmerung*), Wagner allows his characters to engage
in one of the time-honored glories of opera: its ability to portray emotional polyphony through the simultaneous singing
of a trio.

Despite its length, onstage *Götterdämmerung* can seem to flow by with disproportionate rapidity. The final act allows the audience one final oasis as a counterpart to the love scene at the beginning of the opera. Here, as in *Siegfried,* the complementary oasis is nature. The new music of the Rhinemaidens offers a splendid microcosm of the transformations wrought by Wagner's late style. As the horns repeat the basic nature motive from the beginning of *Das Rheingold,* one is tempted to fantasize a tabula rasa, that all can still be made right—despite all the musical evidence to the contrary. The Rhinemaidens' well-known motives of praise for the Rhinegold and their lilting nature song are fully recognizable but surrounded by ravishing curlicues and filigree—a musical counterpart to the Art Nouveau decorative spirit and a prefiguration of the Flower Maidens' music in *Parsifal.* Siegfried's refusal to return the ring replays Brünnhilde's reversal in act one, valuing the ring for its beauty rather than fearing its consequences.

The climactic point of Siegfried's death (track 10) was the original nub for the entire *Ring.* As a result of the tremendous dramatic and musical reconsiderations that have intervened, the scene lacks its originally intended dramatic forcefulness. Wagner attempts to solve the problem through a shift in the center of gravity, by giving the clarifying emotional climax to the purely orchestral commentary of the Funeral March. He pursues a similar strategy, although on a vaster scale, in the final scene, with its concluding orchestral peroration. Siegfried's narration of his earlier exploits entails another twist on the epic recapitulation. Wagner creates a new sense of tension in retelling information the we already know because of the context in which he sets it: as every episode carries us closer to the present, Siegfried's doom approaches. Thus, for example, the ecstatic music associated with discovering Brünnhilde (0:44) suddenly smothers under threatening harmonies (1:10), for it also gives Hagen his cue to strike the hero down (1:29), with his spear, symbolic counterpart to the spear once wielded by Wotan to consolidate his power.

Siegfried's meager dramatic presence—he has never really developed beyond a heroic stick figure—becomes overshadowed by his musical apotheosis in the Funeral March. But he gets one moment to shine brilliantly. Wagner, with apparent irony, accomplishes this with that most hackneyed of gestures, the tenor's death aria (starting at 3:13). The epic recapitulation has set us up to expect, as part of its logical sequence, the music of Brünnhilde's awakening: the music with which the opera itself began. As Siegfried now sings to it, we sense that he too has awakened to a higher consciousness similar to hers. It's as if he realizes now the potential that his life represented and that has now been violently snuffed out. The effect is one of tremendous poignancy, for it serves as a virtual microcosm of the larger *Ring* cycle: we feel we are about to begin again, to face the hope that the two lovers shared when the opera began—but it is all at an end, as Siegfried's phrases fragment into silence (6:45) against the ineluctable fate leitmotif (6:48).

The Funeral March is an even more obvious instance of the shift toward music to carry the burden of meaning. Many have noticed the gulf separating this music's power, and all of its accumulated weight, from the actual hero Siegfried as we've seen him evolve throughout the cycle. The Funeral March itself echoes the C minor pathos of Beethoven's *Eroica* Funeral March. Its network of leitmotifs fashions a kind of hero's shield, on which is inscribed the relevant history of Siegfried: the sad fate of his parents, the promise of the sword, the gleaming heroism of young Siegfried himself, the tormented aspect of Brünnhilde in her humanity. The Funeral March is in the end a purely orchestral equivalent to the epic narratives elsewhere delivered by characters. Its ability to convey an emotional weight even to listeners who come to this episode as absolute music, unaware of the dramatic concatenation leading up to it, presents a fascinating paradox of music's signifying power.

The gripping psychological realism of the transitional scene following is often overlooked, coming as it does between two vast climaxes. Yet the anxiety of Gutrune as she waits for her husband Siegfried to return reminds us of Wagner's skills purely as a musical dramatist, aside from the larger concerns of the *Ring*. It also fleshes out Gutrune's character to the extent that we wish we had seen more of her (Gunther, the brother as easily manipulated as Siegfried by their half-sibling Hagen, never attains this status).

The famous denouement of the cycle, beginning with stagy legerdemain as Siegfried's corpse raises its arm to prevent Hagen from grasping the ring, is left in the hands of Brünnhilde. She now returns for her "Immolation" scene (track 11), which is simultaneously one of the most perplexing yet overwhelming conclusions to a work of art. It's beyond the scope of this overview to rehearse the complicated history of permutations Wagner wrought on the text of her final speech. In themselves, they sum up the array of contradictions and unresolved paradoxes that dogged Wagner throughout the *Ring*'s genesis—"Why does the old world have to end if the ring is returned?" is only the most obvious of these.

In her earlier incarnation, Brünnhilde was a revolutionary coredeemer with Siegfried. The two stormed the barricades of Valhalla to free the world from the curse of greed and usher in a utopia of socialist brotherhood. Wagner's discovery of Schopenhauer then led to a more pessimistic conclusion: that the world can't be redeemed, but we must learn to accept it. Both ideas, with shades in between, are present as part of the opera's "archeology." An analogy from the world of poetry comes to mind that rather neatly encapsulates the basic shift in Wagner's conception. In his poem "September 1, 1939," W. H. Auden originally concluded with the line "We must love one another or die." Later, he confessed that the power of rhetoric had eclipsed logic, and he changed the line to "We must love one another *and* die." The profound change contained in that simple emendation isn't so far from the one exemplified by the *Ring*.

Brünnhilde's final oration is a magnificent culmination. It provides the *Ring*'s ultimate synthesis of epic expansion and dramatic presence. Musically, in addition, it weaves together a great number of key leitmotifs from the cycle's web into a kind of self-contained symphonic poem that recapitulates the story again, but from the perspective of completion. One way to listen to it is simply as a parade of themes, particularly in the final orchestral epilogue. Yet the scene is also filtered through Brünnhilde, and since she has experienced the key events of the *Ring*, her summation of its themes carries our understanding of them to a new level. The scene encapsulates her own evolution and multiple personae: she is lover (2:41), enlightened spirit (6:34), purveyor of forgiveness (7:50), social reformer (8:59), even madwoman (13:01).

Possibly the single most beautiful moment in the entire *Ring* is her address to Wotan, in the passage that literally rocks the theme music of Valhalla to its final rest: "Ruhe, ruhe, Du Gott!" (Rest now, you god!) (7:50). This gentle lullaby, touched with unbearably poignant harmonic coloring (8:02), marks her acceptance of what Wotan had so painfully tried to accept in *Die Walkure:* the relentlessness of the pattern controlling the world. As she returns the ring (its theme reappearing at 9:02) at long last to the Rhinemaidens (9:28), the music begins to coalesce around the primal elements that had begun the cycle. Here it is water; as she prepares to light the funeral pyre and consign Valhalla itself to its fated flames, it is fire (10:51 ff). Loge surges back to full strength from his las-situde in the Norns' scene. Brünnhilde meanwhile turns her attention finally to Siegfried and all he represented, but the chief musical expression is a passionate version of a leitmotif not heard since act 3 of *Die Walküre* (12:42). Then it was sung by Sieglinde as she learned she was pregnant with Siegfried, in praise of Brünnhilde for saving her. Brünnhilde seems to enter into the hallucinatory world we recall from Senta and Isolde in their final scenes. "Siegfried—with joy your wife greets you!" (13:51) are her final words, ending on the energetic and unstable augmented fifth (14:00) of her Valkyrie music.

Wagner had repeated difficulties with the endings of his operas. In one of his earlier letters about the *Ring,* he observed, rather defensively, that the music would have to make things clear: "To make one's intentions too obvious risks impairing a proper understanding of the work in question; in drama—as in any work of art—, it is a question of making an impression not by parading one's opinions but by setting forth what is instinc-tive." Music's language is the solution he chooses for the *Ring.*

But since his very system has set up a connection between that language and the language of drama and ideas, what does the music "say"? After Hagen's last futile attempt to regain the ring (15:04) and the final appearance of the curse motive (in truncated form: 15:06), presumably Alberich is the only one left with desire for its power. The Rhinemaidens reclaim the ring, their innocent nature song (15:21) gives way to the Valhalla theme (15:29), and then a serene version of the Sieglinde leitmotif that Brünnhilde had revived near the end soars above in violins and flutes (15:38). The pattern is repeated (15:45); the Valhalla music is given a final restatement in a series of dramatic modulations (16:02); Siegfried's prophetic theme returns (17:01) and is answered by the last sounding of the gods' downfall leitmotif (17:06); and a descent of a half-step returns to the blissful Sieglinde-Brünnhilde music (17:17). Another indication of Wagner's subtle use of leitmotifs is the very fact that this all-important one has given rise to so much dispute. Its simple lyrical turn contains echoes of a number of wide-ranging motives: the turn in Wotan's farewell, the ornamentation of the Rhinemaidens in act 3, even a phrase from Flosshilde's flirtation with Alberich from the first scene of *Das Rheingold*. This leitmotif is often labeled "redemption by love"; it is also known as the "glorification of Brünnhilde." Both ideas seem to be contained in it: it was announced in response to a message of hope as Sieglinde first sang out the melody. Here it is the response following the music of Valhalla and Siegfried: a message of hope again, that there is a way out of the tragic pattern that resulted in the downfall of both. Even more tellingly, the music comes to rest on a full, swelling D-flat major (17:45). This is not where we began but a step away from the resonant E-flat of the *Rheingold*'s prelude. Why does Wagner's "cycle" not bring us back to where we began?

Here, a phrase from the great Romantic poet Friedrich Hölderlin might offer a clue. His visionary novel *Hyperion* describes the idea of "the eccentric path" (die exzentrische Bahn) that a life takes. He means a kind of spiral upward, which involves repetition of the same patterns but each time with a fuller consciousness of their significance. There is something of this idea in Nietzsche's more famous "eternal return," by which he hopes to come to terms with the constant state of flux of the universe. Wagner seems to suggest, through his very tonality, something similar: the *Ring* is a cycle, the patterns will recur, but we do not arrive back precisely at the point from which we began—if we use the consciousness we have gained.

At the bottom of his final page of the full score, Wagner penned the words "I will write nothing more!" But the greatness of the *Ring* is that there is *always* something more. Wagner's willpower saw him through the creation of one of the most expansive monuments in all the arts, yet more than any of his other works, the *Ring* requires *our* response to be completed. Every generation has its own *Ring*. For all the wonderfully inventive stagings that have been brought to life so far in the *Ring*'s history, the process will of necessity continue.

Made Wise Through Compassion

Wagner's Swan Song *Parsifal*

I f Wagner remains among the most controversial of composers, *Parsifal* is his supreme enigma. The aura surrounding it is unique within the Wagner canon. Some measure of the work's potency might be seen in the contradictory responses it stirs, sometimes even within the same individual. No less a commentator than Nietzsche lavished denunciations, condemning *Parsifal* as "a curse on the senses and the spirit" and "an apostasy and reversion to sickly Christian and obscurantist ideals." Yet when he heard the prelude, he was also moved to praise its "extraordinary sublimity of feeling" and "penetration of vision that cuts through the soul as with a knife.... We get something comparable to it in Dante, and nowhere else."

Nietzsche's conflicting reactions are a kind of paradigm for the intensely charged, diametrical judgments *Parsifal* is still capable of evoking. They have their contemporary echo. On the one hand, some argue that it incorporates the warped ravings of the composer's final years and is therefore inherently pernicious. Others, like Michael Tanner in his book *Wagner,* view *Parsifal* as a work of "peace and conciliation." Such troubling ambivalence is part of the territory when it comes to *Parsifal*. But to let that tempt a newcomer to forego the opera altogether would be a great loss. For when *Parsifal* succeeds, the experience can be as deeply rewarding indeed as Dante, or for that matter *Hamlet* or any other example of the most challenging works of art that might be adduced—creations that have the potential to expand our consciousness.

Parsifal occupies an unusual position in the spectrum of Wagner's life work. In many ways it can be read as a summation. Yet Wagner also clearly considered it *sui generis*. The first thing to notice, however, is *Parsifal*'s intimate, organic connection with the rest of his oeuvre. Adhering to the pattern observed many times before, the opera went through a lengthy gestation period. But the interval between genesis and execution proved to be the widest of all, surpassing even that of the mighty *Ring*. What Wagner referred to in a letter as a process of "ripening" apparently took place both consciously and subconsciously, absorbing the influence of other preoccupations that developed along the way.

This decades-spanning, protracted path toward *Parsifal* in its mature form is reminiscent of Goethe working on *Faust* throughout his lifetime. Aside from some vague earlier encounters, the story first attracted Wagner's serious attention during that extraordinarily fruitful summer vacation of 1845, when he took the water cure at Marienbad to get away from the headaches facing him back in Dresden. Recall that this was the summer that inspired him to turn to *Lohengrin* and that also produced the first sketch for his "lighthearted" comedy *Die Meistersinger*. Included in his reading material was the thirteenth-century epic romance *Parzival* by Wolfram von Eschenbach, the figure who in fact appears as the friendly rival poet in *Tannhäuser*. Wagner later adopted the idiosyncratic spelling "Parsifal" for his work. He was influenced by one of his false etymologies, according to which the name putatively descended from the Arabic *Falparsi* (wise fool). "Parzival" is generally used to refer to Wolfram's romance. Unlike the other ideas that began to crystallize into definite shapes that summer,

Wagner seems to have tucked this away in the back of his mind as a possible source for a new opera.

There it remained—eclipsed by the all-consuming project of the *Ring,* which had taken center stage—until nearly a decade later. It then began to resurface in connection with *Tristan.* Before the latter's scenario had taken its final shape, Wagner actually considered introducing Parsifal into the third act of *Tristan:* lost in his wanderings, he comes upon the wounded Tristan and brings a temporary solace from his pain. Wagner was often attracted to the resonant parallels he saw between characters and situations from several of his music dramas. Indeed, sometimes musical themes do wander between them in place of characters. Tristan's agony carried a clear echo for Wagner of the suffering of one of Wolfram's characters, Amfortas, who would become central to his own treatment of the Parsifal story. Wagner of course abandoned the idea of the Grail knight's guest appearance in *Tristan.*

But the linkage persisted in his musings on the topic. The idea of an entire music drama centered on the Wolfram material began to acquire more definite shape once Wagner found himself ready to begin tackling the musical world of *Tristan.* One of the composer's best-known genesis anecdotes, as recounted in *Mein Leben,* occurs in April 1857 as Wagner is about to move into the "Asyl" at the invitation of his friends the Wesendoncks:

> On Good Friday I awoke to find the sun shining brightly into this house for the first time: the garden was blooming, and the birds singing, and at last I could...enjoy the longed-for tranquility that seemed so fraught with promise. Filled with this sentiment, I suddenly said to myself that this was Good Friday and recalled how meaningful this had seemed to me in Wolfram's *Parzival.* Now its ideality came to me in overwhelming form, and from the idea of Good Friday I quickly sketched out an entire drama in three acts.

As usual, skepticism is required whenever we catch Wagner in the act of self-mythologizing. No such sketch is extant, and commentators have long noted that Good Friday occurred that year weeks before he moved into the new house. But what matters is this epiphany of *Parsifal*'s significance as one deeply connected with Good Friday. It recurs consistently in his references to the still-unwritten work. And it is borne out in *Parsifal* itself, which was created over a decade after Wagner recaptured (or invented) this memory in *Mein Leben*. The paradox of Good Friday—cosmic suffering that coexists with the moment of redemption, of renewed hope—is what matters here. It would prove crucial to Wagner's concept for this music drama.

Several fascinating speculations on the *Parsifal* idea in his private notes and letters to Mathilde Wesendonck, written when he was fully immersed in composing *Tristan* in the late 1850s, reinforce the central role suffering plays in his understanding of the story. One lengthy philosophical epistle Wagner wrote to her contains an unforgettable description of suffering (philosophical epistles were to be expected if one was the object of Wagner's desire). It begins with a detailed account of Wagner passing by a poulterer's shop and witnessing the torments of a hen being slaughtered. The animal's screams, Wagner noted, "transfixed my soul with horror." His lengthy fixation on this scene is reminiscent of Dostoevsky's ruminations on how even the thought of a creature enduring torture is unbearable. From this Wagner segues into a meditation on the phenomenon of suffering and its relation to human consciousness. The sympathy awakened by an animal's helpless suffering is all the more intense because of the animal's inability to transcend its condition. He writes: "[I]f this suffering can have a purpose, it is simply to awaken a sense of fellow-suffering in man, who thereby absorbs the animal's defective existence, and becomes the redeemer of the world by recognizing the error of all existence. (This meaning will one day become clearer to you from the Good Friday morning scene in the third act of *Parzival.*)"

In another letter, Wagner's connection of the Grail epic with suffering, magnified by his currently ongoing portrayal of the hero Tristan, focuses his attention on Amfortas as the pivotal character (rather than Parsifal). The plight of Amfortas, he notes, "is my third-act Tristan inconceivably intensified." An extraordinary description of the extremity of that plight and what it entails even leads Wagner to deplore the idea of tackling the Grail story: "And you expect me to carry through something like this? And set it to music, into the bargain? No thank you very much! I leave that to anyone who has a mind for such things; I shall do all I can to keep my distance from it!"

But Wagner is clearly protesting too much. The more he complains of the absurdity or unsuitability of a particular artistic project he can imagine, the more likely he is to undertake it in the end. The Grail idea had become an obsession. It was a sort of touchstone around which his thoughts would periodically orbit as if steeling himself for the eventual effort of creating this opera. The familiar sense of inevitability—that it was an artistic *necessity* for Wagner to write *Parsifal*—was already present. So was the curious intuition that this would be his swan song, the summation of his entire career.

In the summer of 1865, following the belated premiere of *Tristan* and while he was at work on *Die Meistersinger,* Wagner responded to King Ludwig's request for what he had in mind with his *Parsifal* idea by writing a detailed scenario along with the back story. (*Siegfried's Death* had begun with a detailed scenario of the exposition as well, leading to the *Ring* cycle.) This essentially served as his outline when he turned his full attention to the work twelve years later. He made only one significant change (with regard to the role of the spear that has come into Klingsor's possession).

Although it can certainly be experienced without any prior knowledge of the rest of the Wagner canon, *Parsifal* relates to its predecessors in a kind of interconnected matrix. The density of associations and crossover meanings can seem labyrinthine. Already we've seen the link with Tristan—as a fellow-sufferer, an existential brother to Amfortas. There is a close affinity as well with *Tannhäuser*. Pilgrimage is similarly the prelude to finding salvation, and Wagner consciously worried about repeating himself in the long scene between Parsifal and Kundry (as if he had already "done" this in pairing Tannhäuser with the seductress Venus). These three operas in fact formed a kind of trilogy in Wagner's mind, suitable for being performed in conjunction with one another.

But the connections don't end there. *Der fliegende Holländer,* cursed to a state of wandering, prefigures the time-traveling Kundry who desires the peace of death. Lohengrin, of course, refers to his father Parsifal by name when he is forced to reveal why he has appeared to save the unjustly accused Elsa. His departure tragically underlines the rift between the here-and-now of human desire and the utopian realm of the Grail. The *Ring* contrasts the corruption of Wotan with the innocent Siegfried, a pairing that prefigures Amfortas in his wounded state vis-à-vis the "noble savage" Parsifal. Meanwhile, the original idea of the "Nibelung Hoard," the material analog of the power conferred by the ring, was for Wagner a secular, pagan version of the Christianized Holy Grail. And in *Die Meistersinger,* Sachs's mentoring of Walther mirrors the avuncular patience of Gurnemanz, who eventually realizes (like Sachs) that the mysterious outsider is the path to the future.

Parsifal is, in short, a summation of what is quintessentially Wagnerian. But it's important to realize that at the same time it's unique. Wagner had first to scale other peaks, completing his *Ring* and building his ideal theater, before he could undertake *Parsifal*. And the experience of bringing the *Ring* to the stage, after nearly three decades of tireless effort, had inevitably proved disillusioning. The result was a far cry from the dream of a transfiguring artistic experience. It's as if Wagner then felt the need to start with a clean slate, to dispel the sense of not achieving his ideal in those previous works, by turning again to *Parsifal* in 1877—the year after the world had seen his complete *Ring*.

This time, Wagner was determined to avoid the kinds of compromises he had made in the past by configuring Parsifal specifically for his Bayreuth theater. *Parsifal* is the only work he wrote with the experience of the completed Bayreuth in mind: that fact deeply informs the fabric of the opera, down to the sonority of its scoring. Wagner's desire to set it apart is most evident in the odd new genre name he gave the work: *ein Bühnenweihfestspiel*, which awkwardly translates as "a festival play meant to inaugurate a stage." Wagner's will strictly limited *Parsifal* to performances in Bayreuth, where it would remain unsullied by the compromises of the standard "commercial" opera houses. The Metropolitan Opera's defiance of the copyright embargo and decision to stage *Parsifal* in 1903 caused an international scandal. The composer's widow Cosima took revenge by excommunicating the offending performers from Bayreuth.

Wagner began writing *Parsifal* in 1877, often expressing the belief that this would be his farewell to the opera stage. Many minutiae along the way of its composition (completed in January 1882) have been preserved thanks to Cosima's diaries, which detail progress on the score on an almost daily basis, along with her husband's conversations about its puzzles. Wagner took loving care with every detail. At times he managed just a handful of measures in a single day. The composer's conspicuous penchant for the frills of luxury takes on an added layer of irony in the context of Parsifal. It's hard to resist the image of Wagner surrounded by his silks (an obsession due to his stress-induced and severe erysipelas) and pink satins. He anxiously awaited his expensive perfumes from Paris to calm nerves. Many have relished the counterpoint of this sybaritic indulgence to the ascetic rigors and simplicity of the Monsalvat Wagner's imagination was bringing to life. At the same time, his increasingly fragile health and worsening heart condition while at work on the score have contributed to the impression of weariness that for some is inherent to *Parsifal*. This guilt by association allows the work's detractors to write it off as the species of *fin-de-siècle* decadence in which Nietzsche was the first to cast *Parsifal*.

But there is a more legitimately damning aspect to consider for those who pursue the chords linking the art with the life. The composer's notorious series of essays written during his final years from his new stronghold in Bayreuth cannot be ignored. Wagner had long attracted concentric circles of admirers, in contrast to his vociferous opponents. Bayreuth provided a bastion for the most ardent of these disciples. Among their ranks were truly gifted artists and sensitive souls (including Nietzsche until his dramatic falling out in 1876). But also to be found was a band of obtuse and belligerent "Wagnerians" who established an organ to vent their aggressively nationalist ideology in the journal the *Bayreuther Blätter*.

This was the context in which Wagner produced a string of essays grouped around the theme of "regeneration." Their crackpot, pseudo-Darwinian reflections of racist and anti-Semitic mumbo-jumbo are the most disturbing aspect of Wagner's legacy—and the most offensive alongside his earlier 1850 essay *Judaism in Music*. As a whole, these form an absurd amalgam of the most laughable pseudoscience with bizarrely progressive tendencies. Wagner, quite ahead of his time, passionately advocates animal rights and denounces the cruelty of animal experimentation. Yet he is also capable of constructing a raving theory of primitive man's fall into the original sin of consuming animal flesh, which has exacerbated the inequality of races. Similarly, Wagner considers issues of pacifism and women's rights while blaming the Jews for society's downfall.

The proximity of the toxic elements in these writings to the creation of *Parsifal* is undeniable, a wrenching and disturbing fact. There has been a renewed academic trend to probe this phenomenon with lawyerly meticulousness. And unquestionably some recent critics have yielded worthwhile insights into possible aspects of *Parsifal*. But just as it would be bad faith (however tempting) to ignore the unpleasant penumbra surrounding the opera—or any work of art—perspective is also required in assessing how this fits in with our experience of it. The more extreme camp of Wagner's contemporary detractors tend to read *Parsifal* as nothing but the expression of an esoteric racist theory about "pure blood," as if the opera were a simple allegory or even pamphlet in music. Curiously, they echo, albeit from another angle, the denunciations of *Parsifal* as inherently evil art that were part of its original reception in the 1880s. Such views often disregard the contradictory threads of the libretto and promote a kind of blatant reductionism at least as absurd as pretending there is no dark side to Wagner's genius.

Yet it's important to recall that the scenario of *Parsifal,* in virtually all of its final details, had already been worked out by 1865 (before the nasty "regeneration" pieces). More importantly, the work brings together everything that has concerned Wagner the artist since his voice first emerged. Over time, the response of audiences has attested far more overwhelmingly to its universal qualities than to any hidden, esoteric racism that has to be ferreted out by latter-day skeptics. If there's an overriding lesson in this aspect of the *Parsifal* controversy, it would be that the opera subsumes a complicated, ambivalent texture of coexisting meanings. Ambiguity and indeterminacy, both in a dramatic *and* a musical sense, may well be the real mainspring of *Parsifal's* hold on its audiences' imagination.

In working out his scenario for the story, Wagner reveals an attitude toward his medieval source very similar to what was seen with *Tristan* (indeed, with almost everything since the Dutchman). As he did Gottfried's epic (from which he extracted *Tristan*), Wagner ridicules Wolfram's art. He considers the poet's treatment of the Grail myth an example of the incompetence of an earlier age. His speculations in the letters to Mathilde Wesendonck display a pronounced disdain: "He tacks one event on to the next, one adventure to another, links together the Grail motif with all manner of strange and curious episodes and images, gropes around." In Wolfram's *Parzival,* the posing of a question by the hero is key to the story line. "The thing about the 'question,'" Wagner notes with scorn, "is that it is so utterly preposterous and totally meaningless." In his own reworking of the material, then, *Parsifal* involves an intriguing mixture of *Tristan's* impulse toward abstraction and simplicity with the *Ring's* epic breadth.

Well before the work was ripened, Wagner seems to have fastened on two of its central scenes. They form the great arch of the entire work: the beginning (Amfortas in his plight) and the end (Good Friday morning). Connecting these two points is a long and arduous spiritual pilgrimage—a journey both inner and outer—that Wagner condenses into the confrontations of act 2. As with the murder of Siegfried and the comic picture of Sachs cobbling in competition with Beckmesser's serenade (which provided the kernels, respectively, for the *Ring* and *Die Meistersinger*), the nucleus of *Parsifal* evolves from strikingly visual expressions for its highly abstract ideas. Good Friday's paradox becomes the peaceful blooming of the garden in spring—by Wagner's own account, the image from which his opera originated.

The contrast between suffering humanity and the wise fool who will become its redeemer meanwhile takes the form of Amfortas in the Grail hall as observed by the naïve Parsifal. Lucy Beckett, in her smart and insightful Cambridge Opera handbook *Parsifal,* surmises that the passage in Wolfram's poem where Parzival happens by chance upon Amfortas (spelled "Anfortas" in Wolfram) in the Grail castle was central for Wagner. It was likely an early catalyst for the opera: "Wagner's eye for a scene, a telling stage-picture in which characters are suspended in significance like flies in amber, is fundamental to his genius as a dramatist.... For years he saw Wofram's hall of the Grail, the wounded king, the silent, clumsy boy, and from the picture invented the story which binds the characters together." Interestingly, Wagner's visual sense of *Parsifal*'s deep structure gained confirmation during his travels in Italy during the period of composing the opera. The cathedral in Siena became the prototype for the Grail hall with its Romanesque arcades, while a visit to the garden of the Palazzo Rufolo in Ravello inspired the composer to declare that here was his magic garden (from act 2).

What is it that attracted Wagner so persistently to the Grail story? After all, he deemed his primary source for it in Wolfram's poem hopelessly awkward, a work foreign in sensibility. Our accumulated knowledge about the Grail and its comparative mythology continues to fascinate, filling libraries and web pages. Wagner was also aware, albeit in far less detail, of the broader cultural spectrum of the Grail's core elements. They can be found in ancient, pagan Celtic, and Central Asian sources as well as the more familiar Christian ones, which themselves likely amalgamate an agenda from widespread Christian heresies (as does the Tristan myth). These multiple levels of significance suggest how flexible the story was for Wagner's own artistic purposes.

During the revolutionary fervor that had engendered the *Ring,* Wagner also planned a work called *Jesus of Nazareth.* The following decade, in connection with his Schopenhauer-induced readings in Buddhism, he constructed a scenario for an opera based on a tale of the Buddha's life, *Die Sieger* (The Victors). Both plans, with their accompanying Christian and Buddhist-cum-Schopenhauerian concerns, were able to be subsumed within his *Parsifal.*

Wagner's art continually draws on his understanding of the potency of myth. By the same token, he knows the richness of symbols. The very musical philosophy he had developed expressly for the *Ring* cycle was intended to maximize their effectiveness. *Parsifal* essentially combines these Wagnerian intuitions for myth and symbol. The myth involves the basic story line of the innocent fool who acquires wisdom and thereby solves a crisis. That process of acquiring wisdom requires a trial and a long spiritual journey. It is the prototype for the coming-of-age story (the Bildungsroman, which Thomas Mann, drawing on what he had learned from Wagner, perfected in its twentieth-century incarnation in both *Buddenbrooks* and *Der Zauberberg* [The Magic Mountain]).

The symbol is the powerful Grail, with its overlay of pre-Christian and cross-cultural archetypes. It's not a coincidence that the actual definition of the Grail was hazy and fluid. Wolfram depicts it as a magic stone that becomes the most precious object on earth. Wagner represents the Grail as a chalice: the same one used in the Last Supper to catch the blood of Jesus from the cross. He associates this chalice with the spear that wounds Jesus in his right side. Its separation from the Grail is indeed the catalyst for the situation found at the beginning of *Parsifal.* But Wagner even draws ironic attention to the confusing issue of what the Grail really means, having his young hero formulate his question as "Wer ist der Gral?" (Who is the Grail?). The gaffe actually has more sense to it than a joke illustrating Parsifal's innocent naiveté. F. Owen Lee observes (in his Metropolitan Opera radio broadcast on *Parsifal* published in *First Intermissions*) that this is indeed the ultimate question of the opera: "The Grail that calls out to be redeemed, rescued, restored to wholeness—that is your self, your soul, you."

This conjunction of myth and symbol in a powerful fusion is part of what lends *Parsifal* such tremendous resonance. Wagner's repeated yearning for redemption, expressed in all of its facets from *Der fliegende Holländer* onwards, here reaches its climax. *Parsifal* in fact codifies the redemption myth in a twofold sense. It juxtaposes the hero's epiphany of self-awareness with his capacity to heal Amfortas. The redemption from without must come from within: the myth's truth is reinforced by the potent symbols of the Grail and the Spear (the latter possessing ambivalent connotations for good and evil). Their reunion provides the opera's denouement in a metaphor of healing and wholeness, of yin and yang. Indeed, the very etymology of the word *symbol* from ancient Greek has relevance here. The word refers to a token associated with an individual at birth that becomes split into two pieces; bringing them together again gives proof of the individual's identity.

Wagner's interest in the idea of symbolism can be seen in one of his late essays, *Kunst und Religion* (Art and Religion). Written among the lunacies of the late "regeneration" prose, this essay contains a number of compelling and lucid ideas. The most important (which Wagner sets out at the start in *Art and Religion*) is his claim that "where religion becomes artificial, it is reserved for art to save the spirit of religion by recognizing the figurative value of the mythic symbols which the former would have us believe in their literal sense, and revealing their deep and hidden truth through an ideal presentation." *Parsifal,* in other words, has an intended relationship with the "artificiality" of late-nineteenth-century Christianity (most famously captured in Nietzsche's ironic proclamation that "God is dead").

Wagner's relationship to Christianity is full of confusion and contradictions, a difficult knot to untangle. The young revolutionary was an avowed atheist, thoroughly imbued with the materialism of the era. This was the spirit in which the *Ring* was first conceived, with its overthrow of the corrupt order of gods. Wagner's writings often express hostility to the institutions of organized religion as a corruption of the original spirit of Jesus' teachings, which inspire deep admiration (Wagner at one point pairs Jesus with Apollo as the great teachers of humanity). Jesuits in particular became a bizarre obsession and target of Wagner's vitriol; by the late essays, he castigates them—along with the French—with nearly the degree of invective he applies to Jews. Luther's attempt to return to the "original" Jesus thus held a special allure, yet this easily becomes conflated with an expression of German nationalism (as we see in *Die Meistersinger*). *Parsifal* brings together aspects of Wagner's earlier, humanist appreciation of Christianity with a far more mystical, Catholic outlook in which Christ's suffering bridges the metaphysical rift of being.

But care must be taken (as it must for any aspect of this opera) in addressing the Christian element of *Parsifal.* The tendency to view the opera as a pietistic, sentimental capitulation of nineteenth-century religiosity (Nietzsche's accusation that Wagner at last had "found religion") has lost credence, although this view is in danger of being replaced with an equally saccharine, feel-good New Age "spirituality." There have been compelling and provocative productions that avoid any explicit reference to religion. Nikolaus Lehnhoff's *Parsifal* (staged in San Francisco in 2000) excises all Christian symbology from the stage to focus on a kind of science-fiction quest. This is an extreme position, to be sure. But it reminds us that Wagner himself was worried about the mistaken tendency to view his hero Parsifal as a Christ figure, when he is in fact using Christian symbols—the washing of the feet and anointing in act 3, for example—to uncover their underlying figurative power. If anything, Amfortas in his suffering is closer to Jesus, although his wound is like a stigmata in reverse, a symbol not of holiness and identification but of his failing.

However many-layered and contradictory the strands of meaning in *Parsifal,* Wagner's consistent strategy is to channel them through the powerful, concentrated simplicity of myth and symbol. And with all the wealth of his life's experience to draw on, his music amplifies both directions. It expresses a deep underlying ambiguity *and* it resounds with a clarifying, profound simplicity. This is largely what makes *Parsifal* such a moving but hard-to-assess experience, one that continually shifts over a lifetime of listening. The prelude (CD 1, track 9) is another example of Wagner's preparations for the strange world that is about to unfold. As a sonic entrée, it sets the mood with uncanny aptness from the very first notes. But it also gives the overall impression of a series of questions raised rather than of offering a "synopsis" of the opera. The opening theme (0:01 to 0:48) contains the nucleus of much of the score. It is presented unharmonized, like one long line of chant.

Wagner evokes an archaic—indeed, timeless—atmosphere through metrical uncertainty, draping the melody's quasi-Gregorian simplicity across the barline. It's difficult to determine where the beat lies. The theme's shape is imbued with a symbolic significance. It ascends with a sense of aspiration in a crescendo to a peak where it rises and falls on a semitone (0:16): a virtual microcosm of humanity's striving as a slave to blind Will. Wagner will repeatedly draw attention to this gesture until he pointedly resolves it, in the final pages of the score, with a turn upward to signify the healing that has taken effect. The theme is long, stringing together three separate features that are for the most part presented as discrete entities in the score: the community of the Grail knights united in love as they share the power of the Grail (0:01 to 0:16), the suffering of Amfortas (with that falling semitone; 0:16 to 26), and the Spear (0:28 to 0:32). Pay close attention to Wagner's orchestration as this theme is more fully fleshed out against the strings' arpeggios (1:12 ff). His unusual combinations (oboes and a trumpet for the theme) add an indescribable but piercing poignancy.

Wagner again resorts to diatonic clarity to depict a contrasting order of assurance and renewal in the other two chief themes of the prelude. These are in fact quotations from the past: the famous "Dresden Amen" cadence (5:23), to depict the Grail itself, and a chorale used by Bach, first announced as a fanfare and a leitmotif for the affirmation of faith (6:02). This diatonic simplicity exists through most of the score like a series of islands—temporary refuges—in a sea of roiling, dark complexity, which is the focus of the prelude's last part (10:03 ff). Not until the very end of *Parsifal* do these themes acquire their full significance as a goal, a tonal homecoming.

The harmonies applied to the prelude's opening theme when it is restated in the final part (e.g., 12:21 ff) offer a foretaste of *Parsifal*'s very identifiable sound. There is a thickness here, a harmonic density that is Wagner's expression for the world of Will, illusion, and the suffering that is its only true experience. In accordance with his intuition when first thinking seriously about *Parsifal,* the musical world of *Tristan* seems to be evoked. Indeed, one signature harmony of the opera is a variant of the famous *Tristan* chord, although in a different context, with a different emphasis on its constituent elements. Wagner introduces this angst-ridden harmonic undertow against that striving half-step of the opening theme (13:18 ff) precisely to highlight *Parsifal*'s ambiguity. This is music that can go in the peaceful, resolving direction of the Grail or, just as easily, slide into a morass of suffering and alienation.

Act 1 crystallizes Wagner's earlier vision of the centrality of Amfortas. He had feared that the power of this character would overshadow Parsifal in an uneven polarity. That potential problem, however, is beautifully resolved through Wagner's careful introduction of his hero as an element intruding into the already deeply injured world of the Monsalvat knighthood. Gurnemanz's long exposition, abetted by the unsettling appearance of Kundry, is rudely interrupted as Parsifal enters. His directness and lack of the most basic self-knowledge are a foil to the intense self-awareness that amplifies Amfortas in his suffering. Full musical expression of that suffering seems to reach its peak in the Grail King's magnificent outburst. But even that is overshadowed by the tremendous "Transformation" scene (during the act's scene change), featuring Wagner's miraculous heightening of "filler music" in the mindless march idiom into a sublime outpouring of pain that seems to come from the recesses of Amfortas's wracked consciousness.

The second act presents the "trial" of Parsifal, providing exactly the element of tension that was missing from Wagner's Buddhist project, *Die Sieger*. This tension informs the music in a number of ways, from the sinister chromaticism of Klingsor to the shape-shifting ambiguity of Kundry's motives (with their intriguing connections to the music of Amfortas) and the miragelike, lilting fluidity of the Flower Maidens (a kind of homage paid, some have noted, by the composer to Johann Strauss). The role of this entire act is to prepare for and present the critical moment of transformation within Parsifal. This is a moment reminiscent of the Buddha's attainment of

Enlightenment. As such, it is most effective when the transformation is shown as happening from within.

The first part of the act creates the uncomfortable feeling of Wagner wheeling out creaky old stage machinery. Klingsor can easily come off as a melodramatic villain. Inventive directors have coped with this in a number of ways: Francois Rochaix's Seattle Opera production of 2003, for example, imagined the magician as a ruthless scientist. As Parsifal strays into Klingsor's domain, Wagner resorts to letting the music fill in the gaps where his dramaturgy is wanting. The Flower Maidens immediately entice by virtue of presenting the rare sound of female voices in the score. Their seductive poses meanwhile present a marvelous mock epic (vis-à-vis the armor-clad Parsifal) clueing the audience in to the fact that the battle is going to be a subtle, internal one.

The central scene shows Kundry's attempted seduction. It has led many to exaggerate the role of sexual sin in the world of *Parsifal*—just as sexual desire is easily misread (or underread) in *Tristan*. In some ways, sexual desire (and its taboo) serves as the symbol for the underlying reality Wagner is actually interested in laying bare. That reality, as was made clear in *Tristan,* is the Schopenhauer-inspired vision of endless, tormented longing that can never achieve satisfaction. Indeed, Wagner pointedly quotes the very theme associated with desire from *Tristan* at the crucial moment of Kundry's kiss.

What is of paramount significance in this scene, and in the ultimate trial for the hero, is not his resistance to temptation. That is only the vehicle to something far more central: Parsifal's ability to experience compassion. What Wagner claimed to learn from Schopenhauer was not just a deeply pessimistic vision of life or an aesthetic validation of escape through the powers of music. Wagner was also deeply affected by the philosopher's ethical system and by his understanding of Buddhism, in which compassion for fellow-sufferers—that is, for the entire, hereditary condition of humanity—is the key. The Latin root of the word *compassion,* unlike the more patronizing *pity,* exactly replicates the German term Wagner uses: *Mitleid* or "suffering *with*." The oracular message of the angel recounted in act 1 is musically revived at both obvious and subtle turning points in the drama. It places the concept of compassion in a more specific context: "Durch Mitleid wissend/Der reine Tor/harre sein/den ich erkor" (Through compassion made wise/The holy fool;/Wait for him/Whom I have chosen). Compassion, then, is a form of higher consciousness that can lead us out of current suffering. But it comes at the price of seeing through to the emptiness of existence, in the sense that Wagner had absorbed from Schopenhauer and his understanding of Buddhism.

Kundry's role in enabling Parsifal to attain this state involves one of Wagner's most perfect dramatic inspirations. Indeed, Kundry is arguably his single most fascinating character. She is a conflation of multiple characters from his source material, along with references to figures completely unrelated to Wolfram's epic in the bargain. Kundry represents the cycle of suffering and metempsychosis that underlies reality. Kundry is a female counterpart to the Wandering Jew (and the Dutchman) who has been cursed for laughing at Christ on the cross. She is also a feral child (like Siegfried, and mirroring Parsifal in that regard too), an outsider to the Monsalvat community—in this sense, also a counterpart to Parsifal. And she is the penitent Magdalene.

Marvelously, she seems to wield all these personalities in the pivotal turning point of the opera, where she is foremost the seductress who resorts to all methods available (even exploiting Parsifal's newfound compassionate awareness). Intriguingly, Titian once again served as a muse for this aspect (as he did, by Wagner's account, for the undertaking that became *Die Meistersinger*). The composer specifically refers to the painter's *Venus of Urbino* as a model for Kundry's seductive persona. The extraordinary vocal range Wagner demands of her, from a deep dusky register to piercing shrieks, with quasi-atonal plunges between the two, likewise mirrors Kundry's instability. It is ultimately the psychological challenge she poses for Parsifal that enables his breakthrough; she is the essential foil, not Klingsor (whose music, not surprisingly, is the most weakly conceived and conventional of the opera).

Wagner here enacts what would seem the ineffable: Parsifal's moment of insight. Having witnessed the suffering that Amfortas is condemned to undergo during the Grail ceremony in act 1, Parsifal is now able to understand the origin of that suffering (symbolized by the wound that will not heal). As Wagner had long ago promised Mathilde Wesendonck, the meaning of this enlightenment is to be made clearer in the "Good Friday" scene of the third act.

The prelude to this act is an outstanding tone poem. In just a few minutes, Wagner manages to convey the sense of a pilgrimage through time and through an internal desert of the soul— a pilgrimage far more harrowing than that of Tannhäuser. Like the *Tristan* prelude, it approaches a region of atonality. It also creates the necessary psychological space needed to separate the final act from what has come before. One might even imagine a musical self-portrait here: a distillation of Wagner's long artistic pilgrimage, throughout his career. The most important theme that emerges among these fragments is the one associated with the oracular announcement of the fool enlightened by compassion.

The immense desolation of this music somehow, impossibly, prepares the way for the "Good Friday" scene (CD 1, track 10). We come to realize this is the center of the music drama. It is, even more, perhaps the emotional center of *all* of Wagner's

art: as if his passions, doubts, and hopes have been gravitat-
ing toward this moment. For this scene, in which Gurnemanz
gently explains to Parsifal the paradox of Good Friday, of suffering that can lead to renewal (0:46 ff), is the one moment
when Wagner *depicts* redemption through his art. It is shown
not as a transcendent dream outside this world (the end of *Der
fliegende Holländer* or the *Ring* cycle) but as something that can
be achieved and observed (the faint echo of the rising scalar
melody from the beginning of *Die Meistersinger*'s quintet is perhaps not coincidental [e.g., 0:56]). The beauty of nature is its
representative. Wagner depicts this with the most sensitive
orchestration, with great economy, such as in the delicately
interwoven lines of woodwinds and horns in the spell's waning
moments (3:50 ff). The pleasure of nature becomes shadowed
by a bittersweet quality here, just as so much of *Parsifal*'s
ambiguity plays on the porous division separating pleasure
from pain.

Parsifal brings this moment of enlightenment home in the
final scene, which more formally enacts what the audience
already feels to have occurred: the possibility of Amfortas being
made whole again. Wagner's musical language, however, reinforces this primary experience on a number of levels. The final
pages of the score, with its concentric circles of rising sound in
the chorus, reveal an almost impossibly floating vision of beauty
(again, we are very much in the realm of the *chorus mysticus* of
Goethe's finale to *Faust*). Yet on close hearing, the actual shape
of the music replicates what happens on dramatic and psychological levels. The striving, semitone-bound apex of the Grail
community's theme is now allowed to rise and resolve into a
higher chord. Wagner then brings the resolution home with a
resounding, lush, but fully balanced orchestration of the tonal
center (in A-flat, where *Parsifal*'s prelude had begun). The deli-
cacy combined with majesty here is a microcosm of the score's

remarkable chiaroscuro aspect, its unique ability to blend light and shade, to give the effect of light suddenly flooding in. Wagner's music of suffering has a counterpart in these diaphanous textures. They proved to have an enormous pull on Debussy (just as the harmonic idiom of *Tristan* paves a path toward the German expressionism of Schoenberg and his followers).

The words heard at this point—"Erlösung dem Erlöser" (Redemption to the Redeemer)—are another of *Parsifal*'s great oracles (or mumbo-jumbo, if the work has failed to move one by this point). It seems possible to add continual meanings without exhaustion to what Wagner is attempting to depict here. For one, we recall the kinship between Parsifal and Amfortas that is so pivotal to the second act: there, Parsifal's ability to become a redeemer by recalling Amfortas brings him redemption. And like Lohengrin (his son to be), Parsifal's enlightened status may condemn him to a newfound loneliness—it was Lohengrin just as much as Elsa who needed redemption in Wagner's final "romantic opera."

Yet it's also fascinating to consider Wagner's ongoing tendency toward self-portraiture, as has been seen throughout his life. Only in the *Ring* can one find such an abundance of multiple, contradictory images representing the composer to rival those in *Parsifal*. In the 1980s, the adventurous German film director Hans-Jürgen Syberberg made a famous film of *Parsifal*. His visual concept centered around an enormous replica of Wagner's death mask, upon and in which the action was shown to be taking place. Wagner, by the end of his life, had acquired a following that regarded him as the embodiment of any number of the characters in *Parsifal*. And his legacy indeed combines elements of Parsifal, Amfortas, Kundry, Gurnemanz, even Klingsor (the cheaper thrills of his magical art) into one. *Parsifal* is his attempt to reconcile these, not only for the public, but for himself.

Coda

Wagner's body of work as a whole radiates the powerhouse, cathedral-like sense of solidity that Thomas Mann once defined as archetypical for the nineteenth century. As we've seen, the essential foundation for his canon of operas had already been laid decades before his death. Few artists convey an equivalent image of having fulfilled their artistic mission. We recall Beethoven in his final years declaring that, with his ineffable late quartets, he had only begun to learn how to write music. In contrast, our initial reaction in looking over Wagner's career is one of satisfying completion. For all his misfortunes, ill health, flirtations with suicide, and disastrous miscalculations, Wagner seems to have achieved, against all the odds, what he desired and set out to do.

His own self-doubts about completing the *Ring* or taking on the musico-dramatic challenges of *Tristan* and *Parsifal* at times far eclipsed the constant nay-saying of his most hostile peers. Fantasies of giving it all up and moving to Italy or Brazil or, in his final years, even the United States (on the invitation of a wealthy dentist) are a reminder of the challenges Wagner faced. He once confessed in a letter that "mine is an intensely irritable, acute, and hugely voracious, yet uncommonly tender and delicate sensuality which, one way or another, must be flattered if I am to accomplish the cruelly difficult task of creating in my mind a non-existent world." But ultimately nothing could dam his expressive drive. To top it off, he even managed to get his shrine to the art of the future, the Bayreuth *Festspielhaus,* erected and operational.

Still, an integral aspect of Wagner's legacy is the counter-vailing sense of unfolding discovery afforded by his works, of an unfinished process that can be completed only provisionally, by the shared experience of each new audience. Wagner's art ultimately needs to be appreciated in the opera house as an act of live theater. Anything less can only hint at its unprecedented emotional power and sway—for this is an art that in turn demands visceral reaction rather than passive osmosis from its audience. His famous dictum that those who follow must "create something new" in staging his operas has been predictably used as carte blanche for some truly outrageous glosses. At the same time, Wagnerian opera—like Shakespeare's plays—offers an unusually wide latitude for genuinely innovative interpretation that follows the one essential tenet of authenticity: grounding in and respect for the dramatic and musical text. As just one hypothetical example, it's not farfetched to foresee a *Ring* that situates the so-called Vulcan war cabinet of the George W. Bush administration in Valhalla or the ruthless terrorism of the Qaida network as a figure for the never-ending power stuggles embodied in the cycle.

Even considering the music as an element apart from the rest, it's not by chance that Wagner's is not the kind easily commodified for use as a pleasant acoustic background wash in malls and airports. Wagner discovered a way to access and express levels of feeling so unerringly that, with no background in music or the opera stories themselves, a listener often gains an intuitive grasp of some underlying meaning. Most artists are myopic to the extent of focusing solely on their particular artistic space. But Wagner saw his art as a mere means to the vaster end of understanding an alienated world and creating meaning in it. This approach is, of course, one extreme point on the rich spectrum of the role art is able to play in our lives. We would be immeasurably impoverished to consider it the only one—indeed, Wagner himself seems to have realized this. To forget how his art fits into such a spectrum results in the loss of perspective responsible for many of the original controversies swirling about Wagnerism.

To adapt Isaiah Berlin's famous application of the ancient aphorism: the fox who knows many things, not the single-minded hedgehog, shows us how to approach this artist. Wagner was the epitome of the shape-shifter. In *The Sorrows and Grandeur of Richard Wagner*—arguably the single most penetrating overview of the composer ever written—Thomas Mann notes that this is the kind of artist who "surrenders himself to the changing physiological moods of each period of his life, representing them in works that contradict each other intellectually, but that are all beautiful and worthy of preservation."

What constituted a wily and disagreeable trait in his character has a positive and richly rewarding correlative in his art: for his greatest music dramas are not mere reflections of self-absorption, mirrors of a monstrous ego. They absorb Wagner's conflicting dimensions and amalgamate these into monumentally stirring meditations on the contradictory range of human experience. Inspired by an idiosyncratic, idealistic view of the significance of art—above all, the communal theater festivals—in ancient Greek culture, Wagner denounced the devolution of contemporary opera into a formulaic commodity meant to provide frivolous entertainment. The core element of Wagner's creative struggle centered around his elevation of the work of art to an ultraserious role intended to unfold humanity's deepest truths and thus transport its audience into a higher state of consciousness. And the goal, from first to last—the source, indeed, of all his contradictions—was the longing for redemption and peace.

Reflecting on what he had really meant for the century that he dominated, Debussy once remarked that had Wagner only been "a little more human," he would have been entirely great. The impulse to separate the flawed human from the artwork is especially intense, but it leads to particularly noisome confusion in the case of Wagner. In the end, the contradictions and tensions embodied in his art point to something more potentially transforming than we have become used to expecting from the world of entertainment. And the most eloquent testimony thereof is the simple fact that this diminutive man could conceive and carry out the art he left to us.

Wagner spent his final days in Venice. In the land where—by his own report—he had first conceived the music to begin the *Ring* cycle, and in the city where he had composed an essential part of *Tristan,* he died in early 1883. Exile, in a sense, was a state from which Wagner never managed to escape, for all the contradictory blustering of his later nationalism. Without his interior experience of exile—Wagner's deep, wounding alienation from the society around him—the art never would have been born. To it even more than to the theatrically oversize egomania and tireless self-promotion that have become inseparable from his reputation do we owe the creation of works that reach far beyond their mooring in the preoccupations of the nineteenth century to challenge us today and in the future.

Chronology

1813	Richard Wagner born in Leipzig on May 22.
1814	His mother, Johanna, marries Ludwig Geyer, following the death of her first husband.
1821	Death of his beloved stepfather, artist-actor Ludwig Geyer.
1828	Finishes script of his Gothic tragedy *Leubald*. Decides to undertake serious study of composition. His first pieces, written in the next few years, focus on instrumental genres.
1830	Passion for Beethoven evident from his piano transcription of the Ninth Symphony (premiered in 1824).
1831	Begins study at Leipzig University.
1832	First opera, *Die Hochzeit,* is conceived but then abandoned.
1833	Obtains first professional job as chorus master in Würzburg. Begins his first completed opera, *Die Feen* (finished in January 1834 but unperformed).

1834–1836	Takes post as music director of traveling theater company operating out of Magdeburg. Conceives idea for next opera, *Das Liebesverbot,* in summer of 1834 (completed in 1836). Meets Christine Wilhelmine Planer ("Minna") later that summer.
1836	Marries Minna and moves with her to new post at Königsberg.
1837–1839	Music director for theater in Riga. Conceives *Rienzi* (begun in 1838, completed in 1840 in Paris).
1839	Massive debts force him to flee with Minna in dramatic exodus from Riga. Stormy voyage through North Sea later claimed to inspire idea for *Der fliegende Holländer.*
1839–1842	Miserable years of poverty in Paris. Odd jobs as arranger. Writes prose pieces and fiction.
1840	Begins composing *Der fliegende Holländer* in May (completed in November 1841).
1842	Premiere of *Rienzi* in October a massive triumph in Dresden.
1843–1849	Position as Kapellmeister in Dresden. Premiere of *Der fliegende* Holländer there in January 1843. During this period, intensely active as conductor. Extensive reading in classical literature, Germanic mythology, politics, and philosophy.
1843	Begins *Tannhäuser* (completed in April 1845).

1845   Summer holiday in Marienbad proves font of
                inspiration: conceives *Lohengrin* (composed
                between 1846 and 1848; premiered in Wagner's
                absence under Liszt in Weimar in 1850) as well
                as first inklings of *Die Meistersinger* and *Parsifal*.
                Tannhäuser premiered in October.

1848   Death of his mother, Johanna. First detailed
                prose scenario in October for drama that will
                become *Ring* cycle.

1849   European Revolution arrives in Dresden. Wagner
                participates in organizing activities. Warrant for
                his arrest issued in May. Flees to Switzerland.
                Makes Zurich his new home in the summer.
                Writes *Art and Revolution* and *The Artwork of
                the Future*.

1850–1853   Continues focus on theoretical writings, in par-
                ticular on his vision for music theater in *Opera and
                Drama*. Publishes notoriously anti-Semitic essay
                Judaism in Music in fall 1850. Begins sketches
                for *Siegfrieds Tod* and expands the *Ring* into a
                tetralogy.

1853   Publishes first complete edition of *Ring* texts.
                Epiphany at La Spezia, Italy, entailing first
                musical vision for the *Ring* (according to *Mein
                Leben*). Begins *Das Rheingold* (score completed in
                September 1854).

1854   Begins composing *Die Walküre* (score completed
                in March 1856). Discovers Schopenhauer's phi-
                losophy in the fall. Announces idea for *Tristan*
                opera.

1855   Concert tour in London.

1856   Begins composing *Siegfried* (score not completed
              until 1869).

1857   Wesendoncks invite Wagners to move into cot-
              tage on their estate outside Zurich (the "Asyl").
              Love for Mathilde Wesendonck deepens. In
              spring (supposedly on Good Friday), inspired to
              write detailed scenario for *Parsifal*. Puts *Siegfried*
              aside after finishing act 2 in summer. Begins
              work on *Tristan und Isolde* (score completed in
              August 1859).

1858   Crisis at the "Asyl." Escapes to Venice to continue
              work on Tristan.

1859–1861   Relocates to Paris after completing *Tristan* in
              Lucerne. Extensively revises *Tannhäuser* for Paris
              premiere, which is a fiasco.

1861   Decides during a trip to Venice in November to
              write *Die Meistersinger*.

1862   Granted full amnesty to return to German soil.
              Resettles in Biebrich on the Rhine and devotes
              himself to writing *Die Meistersinger* (score com-
              pleted in October 1867). Final separation from
              Minna.

1863   Concert tours in Russian and Eastern Europe.
              Lodges for a time in Vienna. Wagner and Cosima
              pledge their love in November.

1864   Another crisis drives Wagner to a low point.
              Debts force him to flee Vienna. Dramatic turn in
              fortunes as King Ludwig II of Bavaria ascends the

throne in March. He begins support of Wagner, moving him into luxurious accommodations in Munich.

1865   Premiere of *Tristan* in June under Cosima's husband Hans von Bülow. Begins autobiography *Mein Leben*. Comes under attack from faction of Ludwig's court and flees Munich.

1866–1872   Relatively happy years with Cosima in new home in Tribschen on Lake Lucerne. Minna dies in 1866. Marries Cosima in August 1870.

1868   June premiere *of Die Meistersinger* in Munich is a triumph.

1869   Returns to work on the *Ring* in March, taking up act 3 of *Siegfried* (score completed in February 1871). Begins composing *Götterdämmerung* in October (score completed in November 1874). Friendship with Friedrich Nietzsche develops (they break in 1876).

1871   Selects Bayreuth as site for his *Festspielhaus.*

1872   Foundation ceremony for Bayreuth theater on Wagner's birthday (May 22), including performance of Beethoven's Ninth. Wagner and Cosima relocate to Bayreuth.

1874   Moves into Bayreuth home, Villa Wahnfried. Rehearsals for *Ring* cycle begun. Completes final page of *Götterdämmerung* score on November 21.

1876   World premiere of entire *Ring* cycle at first Bayreuth Festival in August. (*Das Rheingold* had been premiered separately in Munich in 1869,

Die Walküre in 1870, under Ludwig's orders and against Wagner's vehement objections). Huge debt incurred. Beginning of Wagner's romantic liaison with Judith Gautier.

1877   Begins composing *Parsifal* in September (completed in January 1882).

1878–1881   Final series of prose writings, ranging from antivivisectionist campaign to a series of racist and anti-Semitic "regeneration" essays for the *Bayreuther Blätter* journal.

1882   *Parsifal* premiered at Bayreuth Festival on July 26 under Hermann Levi. Family takes up residence at the Palazzo Vendramin in Venice in September.

1883   Begins unfinished essay on the "eternal feminine." Dies in Venice on February 13.

A Basic Glossary

absolute music
Wagner's catch-all phrase for music as an end in itself. An integral phase of evolution in Western music that reached its culmination with Beethoven, whose Ninth Symphony anticipates for Wagner the need to integrate music and speech at a higher level. In his own day, **absolute music** could be found in the frivolous showpieces of opera as well as, more obviously, the futile attempts to persist with exhausted instrumental forms (supposedly exemplified by Brahms). Wagner's own later work reveals a new attitude toward music (influenced by its role in Schopenhauer's philosophy) as the predominant element in his art.

art of transition
Wagner's assessment of his "most delicate and profound art" and the "secret of my musical form," applied to his achievement in *Tristan* (especially act 2) as described in a letter to Mathilde Wesendonck. The careful gradation—which is to register subliminally to the spectator—from one emotional extreme to another through specific musical devices and dramatic planning, achieving unity over a large expanse of time.

bar form   AAB form, (also called *Abgesang*), one of the
                           traditional song forms of the Meistersinger
                           and an explicit topic in the discussions of
                           art within *Die Meistersinger,* where Wagner
                           reclaims the closed song-form that had been
                           banished from the rigorous idea of the **music
                           drama** but was essential to old-fashioned
                           number opera. Walther's "Prize Song" is in
                           AAB form: its first two stanzas follow the same
                           melody, while the third (as in Hegelian dialec-
                           tic) combines elements of the two into a new
                           melody. Sachs uses the metaphor of a man and
                           woman who unite to have a child. Musicologist
                           Alfred Lorenz, responding to widespread cri-
                           tiques that Wagner's art elevates content into
                           formlessness, hypothesized that the acts of the
                           music dramas themselves are modeled on the
                           bar form on a vast scale (for example, the
                           three acts of *Die Meistersinger* create an AAB
                           form). This, he claims, is the "secret of form"
                           in Wagner's music.

Bayreuth   Wagner's dream-come-true of a state-of-
                           the-art theater dedicated to the most serious
                           art (that is, his own). A result of his life-long
                           idealization of classical Greek art, envisioned
                           as a way to revive the ancient dramatic festivals
                           in which the community was drawn together,
                           and a solution to the entertainment focus of
                           contemporary theaters and opera houses.
                           The concept of a special "festival theater"
                           (*Festspielhaus*) went hand in hand with the
                           genesis of the *Ring.* His original idea was for a
                           kind of proto-Woodstock, a temporary theater
                           where communal bliss would prevail. After
                           much searching, Wagner settled on the small

Bavarian town of **Bayreuth** to locate his the-ater, which was inaugurated with the premiere of the *Ring* in 1876. Wagner's original intent was for open admission to anyone who desired to make the pilgrimage, along with a music and theater school dedicated to the art of perfor-mance. His egalitarian ideas did survive in the design of the house itself, which replaces orna-mentation, the classicist division into boxes, and so forth with a functionalist model drawn from the Greek amphitheater. The design of the covered pit to make the orchestra "invis-ible" was another radical feature to enhance the experience of the music drama. The Bayreuth Festival continues with performances every summer—and has become one of the most hard-to-get tickets in the world.

bel canto

Literally "beautiful singing"—the style devel-oped to perfection by the early Romantic Italian masters of opera (Donizetti, Bellini, Rossini). Wagner's attitude was typically ambivalent. He was exposed to a great deal of this style in his own work as a repertory opera conductor. On the one hand, it comes to signify a useless attachment to **absolute music** at the expense of drama. Yet Wagner remained an admirer of Bellini's approach to melody and emulated it in numerous ways. The presence of the **bel canto** style as an element of Wagner's own conception of good singing is being recaptured by some performers today.

Bühnenweihfestspiel

Wagner's term for *Parsifal*'s genre: literally, a "festival play meant to inaugurate a stage." The **Bayreuth** stage had of course already been inaugurated before the premiere of Parsifal in

1882 with the first performance of the *Ring* cycle, termed by Wagner a "stage festival play" in homage to the great theater festivals of the ancient Greeks.

eternal feminine   A central Romantic concept most famously codified in the final chorus of Goethe's *Faust*, Part II ("das ewig-Weibliche/zieht uns hinan"). Faust's redemption has been secured through "the **eternal feminine,** which draws us upward"—the feminine here referring to the power of love as manifest in woman. In connection with Wagner, this is too often confused with the woman-on-a-pedestal clichés of the later nineteenth century. Wagner's typically intense approach to the **eternal feminine** as involving a love both compassionate and self-sacrificing in fact infuses his characters (most notably Brünnhilde) with a richness and complexity that can't be reduced to a simple formula.

Gesamtkunstwerk   From Wagner's theoretical treatises, the concept of a complete or "total art work" that reunites the individual arts once integrated in the work of the ancient Greeks and since fragmented by the pressures of specialization and commercial attitudes. The chief arts to be "recombined" are music, poetry, and dance, into an integral unity that is the work of drama. (Wagner's emphasis on dance might seem curious, considering his distaste for the ballet of French grand opera; it's helpful to think of it as allied to the function of rhythmic expression, as in Beethoven's Seventh Symphony, famously labeled by Wagner "the apotheosis of the dance.") Wagner considers the role of other more technical elements as well—stage design, acting gestures—in the complete artwork. Its reception by the audience is moreover crucial to its identity, for the vision is not of "art for art's sake" but of an engaged, revolutionary art that can transform society.

Heldentenor

Literally "heroic tenor": the uniquely powerful vocal style required for Wagner's strenuous roles (especially Siegfried and Tristan). Wagner's dramatic expansion of the orchestra's role from its subservience in traditional opera created a need for a special kind of singer. At its worst, this devolved into the so-called Bayreuth bark—the unpleasant vocal aggressiveness of more recent decades that ignored the **bel canto** element in Wagner's vocal thinking.

leitmotif (also spelled *leitmotiv*)

Literally "leading motive": probably the most famous term connected with Wagner's music. Wagner himself didn't use the term, nor did he invent the concept of musical ideas or figures that recur and are associated with a character or dramatic idea (such as the D minor chords for the Stone Guest in Mozart's *Don Giovanni*). But Wagner did take this concept far beyond what had been imagined previously. He developed it into a remarkably organic structure as the basic tissue of his musical fabric. His earliest works anticipate the **leitmotif,** but its enormous dramatic and psychological potential comes to fruition in the post-*Lohengrin* works, above all the *Ring* cycle, where it is used to shape and give unity to the vast fifteen-hour work. Wagner carefully delineated the leitmotif's theoretical aspects in *Opera and Drama*, identifying various classes such as "motives of anticipation" and "motives of reminiscence." The leitmotif is often parodied as a kind of musical business card, but Wagner's manipulation of its associative character and symphonic potential is one of the hallmarks of his genius.

music drama A term often used rigidly to separate Wagner's art from traditional opera and meant to convey the lofty aims he developed for his brand of opera, as elaborated in *Opera and Drama* and other writings. Wagner's evolution, very generally, was from a vision of the "total artwork," in which the drama was the predominant end. Subordinate to it were music and poetry—in fact all the combined arts were merely means to heighten the experience of this end. The drama was the result of the "musico-poetic" inspiration (that is, both music and poetry were considered inseparable in its origin) and was meant to be experienced by the audience as such. Later, Wagner's attitude began to elevate the musical element again when he characterized his works as "deeds of music made visible." Nowadays, there's really no reason not to use the terms *opera* and **music drama** interchangeably.

mythos Wagner's term for archetypal story lines and the truths they reveal. In contrast to the rococo use of classical myth, which had a strong presence in many of the opera plots of the past, Wagner approached myth as a repository of infinite potential that was best grasped when distracting plot lines were pared down to essential simplicity (most famously, in the "soul states" of his version of *Tristan*). Myth, unlike the rigid, confusing stories of historical opera, offers a "plasticity" (one of Wagner's favorite words for artistic shaping) especially conducive to the aims of the **Gesamtkunstwerk.** Myth is closely allied to symbol and to Wagner's view of religion and its use of symbols in *Parsifal*.

number opera   A type of opera in which the music is divided up into discrete "numbers" or set pieces, such as arias, duets, trios, and so forth up through choruses. In between these numbers (which can often be readily excerpted for performance outside the opera), the plot is advanced through the semi-sung dialogue of recitative (which tends to follow the patterns of speech). As with musical comedy, the action tends to pause when the numbers begin as the characters reflect on their current situation. In its heyday in the eighteenth century, the **number opera** proved exceedingly amenable to both baroque and classical styles. But it was already beginning to seem obsolete in Wagner's time. His mature works strive for a seamless texture in which there is no longer any distinction between "dialogue" and "number" (hence the famous phrase "bleeding chunks" for attempts to excerpt musical scenes from Wagnerian opera). But even here occasionally can be found traces of the old-fashioned number division. And conversely, it's important to realize that composers who worked within the **number opera** mold often found ingenious means to create extended dramatic sequences (in particular, Mozart), while

Wagner's contemporary Verdi created his own remarkable synthesis of set numbers and richly composed dramatic dialogue. As a reaction to Wagnerism, twentieth-century neoclassicists deliberately revived the **number opera** (as did Stravinsky in *The Rake's Progress*).

redemption

As Nietzsche observed, the overriding preoccupation of Wagner's art—a religious term (*Erlösung*), which was co-opted for Wagner's peculiar vision of art as religion. Wagner's need to dramatize **redemption** emphasizes the degree of alienation that he constantly experienced. It variously applies to social transformation via revolution (the *Ring*), overcoming the drive of the will through renunciation (*Tristan*), valuing the beauty of art (*Die Meistersinger*), and a combination of all of these through the vision of compassion for universal suffering (*Parsifal*). Also recurrent to the idea of **redemption** is the role of love, often in sacrifice, as the only power to counter the warped values of society. Such love is the gift of a compassionate woman (influenced by the pervasive idea of the "**eternal feminine**" that "drives us upward" from the end of Goethe's *Faust*).

Stabreim

The highly alliterative style of verse that Wagner pursued in particular in his *Ring* librettos and based on a mistaken belief in the folk origin of some of the poetic sources Wagner used in his research. The effect of Wagner's alliterative patterns, coupled with his emphasis on relations between word roots, is of a pseudo-archaic speech.

Wahn

A word richly resonant with personal associations for Wagner and, in a sense, a sense, his slant to Schopenhauer's idea of the blind **Will.** Wahn implies illusion and the folly that guides human behavior, as well as the emptiness of vanity—perhaps akin to the "life lie" in Ibsen's plays. It's the central theme of Hans Sachs's great act 3 monologue in *Die Meistersinger.* Wagner called his final home in **Bayreuth** "Wahnfried," an ambivalent name that could mean either "freedom from illusion" or "illusion's peace."

Will

The all-important concept of Schopenhauer's philosophy, influenced by his reading of German idealism cross-fertilized with Eastern and Buddhist ideas. Will is the ultimate basis for reality and is the irrational, purposeless life force, the source of suffering that subjects all creatures to a kind of hamster wheel of useless striving. Recognition of the **Will**'s presence is the first step toward achieving the nirvana of negation of desire.

Bibliography and Suggested Reading

Adorno, Theodor. 1991. *In Search of Wagner.* Trans. Rodney Livingstone. Reissue ed. New York: Verso Books.

Becket, Lucy. 1981. *Parsifal. Cambridge Opera Handbooks.* New York: Cambridge University Press.

Dahlhaus, Carl. 1992. *Richard Wagner's Music Dramas.* Trans. Mary Whittall. New York: Cambridge University Press.

Deathridge, John, and Carl Dahlhaus. 1997. *New Grove Wagner.* Rev. ed. New York: W.W. Norton.

De Rougemont, Denis. 1983. *Love in the Western World.* Trans. Montgomery Belgion. Princeton: Princeton University Press.

Donington, Robert. 1984. *Wagner's Ring and Its Symbols.* 3rd ed. London: Faber & Faber.

Gregor-Dellin, Martin. 1983. *Richard Wagner: His Life, His Work, His Century.* Trans. New York: Harcourt.

Gutman, Robert. 1968. *Richard Wagner: The Man, His Mind, and His Music.* New York: Harcourt.

Hanslick, Eduard. 1950. *Music Criticisms: 1846–99.* Trans. and ed. Henry Pleasants. New York: Penguin Books.

Hartford, Robert, ed. 1980. *Bayreuth: The Early Years: An Account of the Early Decades of the Wagner Festival as Seen by Celebrated Visitors and Participants.* New York: Cambridge University Press.

Lee, M. Owen. 2002. *First Intermissions: Commentaries from the Met Broadcasts.* New York: Limelight Editions.

Lee, M. Owen. 1994. *Wagner's Ring: Turning the Sky Around.* New York: Limelight Editions.

Magee, Bryan. 1988. *Aspects of Wagner.* New York: Oxford Press.

Magee, Bryan. 2001. *The Tristan Chord: Wagner and Philosophy.* New York: Metropolitan Books.

Magee, Elizabeth. 1991. *Richard Wagner and the Nibelungs.* Oxford, U.K.: Clarendon Press.

Mann, Thomas. 1986. *Pro and Contra Wagner.* Trans. Erich Heller. Chicago: University of Chicago Press.

Millington, Barry, ed. 2001. *The Wagner Compendium.* London: Thames & Hudson.

Millington, Barry, and Stewart Spencer, ed. 1992. *Wagner in Performance.* New Haven: Yale University Press.

Millington, Barry. 1992. *Wagner.* Rev. ed. Princeton: Princeton University Press.

Müller, Ulrich, and Peter Wapnewski, ed. 1992. *Wagner Handbook.* Trans. ed. John Deathridge. Cambridge: Harvard University Press.

Newman, Ernest. 1991. *The Wagner Operas.* Reprint ed. Princeton: Princeton University Press.

Nietzsche, Friedrich. 1994. *The Birth of Tragedy from the Spirit of Music.* Trans. Shaun Whiteside. Ed. Michael Tanner. New York: Penguin Books.

Nietzsche, Friedrich. 2000. *Basic Writings.* Trans. Walter Kaufmann. New York: Modern Library.

Sadie, Stanley, ed. 1999. *Wagner and His Operas (New Grove Composers Series).* New York: St. Martin's Press.

Shaw, George Bernard. 1967. *The Perfect Wagnerite.* 4th ed. Mineola, N.Y.: Dover Publications.

Spotts, Frederic. 1996. *Bayreuth: A History of the Wagner Festival.* New Haven: Yale University Press.

Tanner, Michael. 1996. *Wagner.* Princeton: Princeton University Press.

Wagner, Cosima. 1997. *Cosima Wagner's Diaries: An Abridgement.* Trans. Martin Cooper. Ed. Geoffrey Skelton. Reprint ed. New Haven: Yale University Press.

Wagner, Richard. 2000. *My Life.* Trans. Andrew Gray. Reprint ed. New York: Da Capo Press.

Wagner, Richard. 1995. *Opera and Drama.* Trans. William Ashton Ellis. Lincoln: University of Nebraska Press.

Wagner, Richard. 1994. *Religion and Art*. Trans. William Ashton Ellis. Lincoln: University of Nebraska Press.

Wagner, Richard. 1983. *The Ring of the Nibelung*. Trans. Andrew Porter. New York: W. W. Norton.

Wagner, Richard. 1988. *Selected Letters of Richard Wagner*. Trans. Stewart Spencer. Ed. Barry Millington. New York: W.W. Norton.

Wagner, Richard. 1988. *Wagner on Music and Drama: A Compendium of Prose Works*. Ed. Evert Sprinchorn and Albert Goldman. New York: Da Capo Press.

CD Track Listing

CD 1

1. *Der fliegende Holländer*: Overture (10:07)
   Adrian Leaper, conductor, Orquesta Filarmonica de Gran Canaria
   ℗ 1995 Arte Nova Musikproduktions GmbH. Courtesy of the RCA Victor Group, a unit of BMG Music.
   From *Orchestral Highlights*, Richard Wagner, Arte Nova Classics-BMG Classics, 74321 56360 2.

2. *Tannhäuser*: Elisabeth's Greeting (*"Dich, teure Halle"*) (4:07)
   Sabine Passow, soprano; Ivan Anguelov, conductor, Stuttgart Philharmonic
   ℗ 1999 Arte Nova Musikproduktions GmbH. Courtesy of the RCA Victor Group, a unit of BMG Music.
   From *Sabine Passow, Portrait*, Arte Nova Voices, Arte Nova Classics-BMG Classics, 74321 67516 2.

3. *Lohengrin*: Prelude (8:23)
   Sir Colin Davis, conductor, Bavarian Radio Symphony
   ℗ 1995 BMG Music. Courtesy of BMG Classics, a unit of BMG Music.
   From *Ben Heppner Sings Lohengrin*, RCA Red Seal-BMG Classics, 09026-68239-2.

4. *Lohengrin*: Lohengrin's Grail Narration (*"In fernem Land"*) (6:02)
   Ben Heppner, tenor; Sir Colin Davis, conductor, Bavarian Radio Symphony
   ℗ 1995 BMG Music. Courtesy of BMG Classics, a unit of BMG Music.
   From *Ben Heppner Sings Lohengrin*.

5. *Tristan und Isolde*: Prelude (11:25)
   Adrian Leaper, conductor, Orquesta Filarmonica de Gran Canaria
   ℗ 1995 Arte Nova Musikproduktions. Courtesy of the RCA Victor Group, a unit of BMG Music.
   From *Orchestral Highlights*, Richard Wagner.

6. *Tristan und Isolde*: Liebestod (*"Mild und leise"*) (7:08)
   Leontyne Price, soprano; Henry Lewis, conductor, Philharmonia Orchestra
   ℗ 1980 BMG Music. Courtesy of BMG Classics, a unit of BMG Music.
   From *The Prima Donna Collection: Leontyne Price*, RCA Gold Seal-BMG Classics, 09026-61236-2.

7. *Die Meistersinger*: Sachs's Act 3 Monologue (*"Wahn, Wahn"*) (6:28)

Otto Wiener, bass; Joseph Keilberth, conductor, Bavarian State Orchestra

Originally recorded prior to 1972. All rights reserved by BMG Music. Courtesy of BMG Ariola Classics GmbH.

From *Die Meistersinger von Nurnberg*, Richard Wagner, eurodisc-BMG Classics, GD69008.

8. *Die Meistersinger*: Walther's Prize Song (*"Morgenlich leuchtend"*) (5:40)

Robert Dean Smith, tenor; Ivan Anguelov, conductor, Slovak Radio Symphony

℗ 2000 Arte Nova Musikproduktions GmbH. Courtesy of the RCA Victor Group, a unit of BMG Music.

From *Robert Dean Smith, Wagner Portrait*, Arte Nova Voices, Arte Nova Classics-BMG Classics, 74321 81176 2.

9. *Parsifal*: Prelude (15:24)

Arturo Toscanini, conductor, NBC Symphony Orchestra

Originally recorded prior to 1972. All rights reserved by BMG Music. Courtesy of BMG Classics, a unit of BMG Music.

10. *Parsifal*: "Good Friday Spell" (*Charfreitagszauber*) (4:51)

Albert Dohmen, bass-baritone; Stefan Anton Reck, conductor, Orchestra del Teatro Massimo Palermo

℗ 2001 Arte Nova Musicproduktions, GmbH. Courtesy of the RCA Victor Group, a unit of BMG Music.

From *Albert Dohmen, Wagner Portrait*, Arte Nova Voices, Arte Nova Classics-BMG Classics, 74321 90063 2.

CD 2
Excerpts from the *Ring*

Marek Janowski, Conductor, Staatskapelle Dresden

From *Der Ring des Nibelungen*, Richard Wagner, RCA Red Seal-BMG Classics, 82876 55709 2.

1. *Das Rheingold*: Prelude (3:51)

℗ 1980 BMG Music. Courtesy of BMG Ariola Classics GmbH.

2. *Das Rheingold*: Entrance of the Gods into Valhalla (7:39)

Eberhard Büchner, tenor (Froh), Peter Schreier, tenor (Loge), Theo Adam, bass-baritone (Wotan), Lucia Popp, soprano, Uta Priew, mezzo-soprano, Hanna Schwarz, alto (Rhinemaidens)

℗ 1980 BMG Music. Courtesy of BMG Ariola Classics GmbH.

3. *Die Walküre*: First meeting: Siegmund and Sieglinde (5:00)
   Siegfried Jerusalem, tenor (Siegmund), Jessye Norman, soprano (Sieglinde)
   ℗ 1981 BMG Music. Courtesy of BMG Ariola Classics GmbH.

4. *Die Walkure*: Ride of the Valkyries (5:33)
   ℗ 1981 BMG Music. Courtesy of BMG Ariola Classics GmbH.

5. *Die Walkure*: Wotan's Farewell and Magic Fire Music (15:22)
   Theo Adam, bass-baritone (Wotan)
   ℗ 1981 BMG Music. Courtesy of BMG Ariola Classics GmbH.

6. *Siegfried*: Siegfried's Forging Song (3:52)
   René Kollo, tenor (Siegfried), Peter Schreier, tenor (Mime)
   ℗ 1982 BMG Music. Courtesy of BMG Ariola Classics GmbH.

7. *Siegfried*: Forest Murmurs (2:31)
   René Kollo, tenor (Siegfried)
   ℗ 1982 BMG Music. Courtesy of BMG Ariola Classics GmbH.

8. *Siegfried*: Siegfried and Brünnhilde/Love Duet (6:06)
   René Kollo, tenor (Siegfried), Jeannine Altmeyer, soprano (Brünnhilde)
   ℗ 1982 BMG Music. Courtesy of BMG Ariola Classics GmbH.

9. *Götterdämmerung*: Hagen's Watch (3:40)
   Matti Salminen, bass (Hagen), Siegmund Nimsgern, bass-baritone (Alberich)
   ℗ 1983 BMG Music. Courtesy of BMG Ariola Classics GmbH.

10. Götterdämmerung: Siegfried's Death (7:01)
    René Kollo, tenor (Siegfried), Matti Salminen, bass (Hagen)
    ℗ 1983 BMG Music. Courtesy of BMG Ariola Classics GmbH.

11. *Götterdämmerung*: Brünnhilde's Immolation (18:09)
    Jennine Altmeyer, soprano (Brünnhilde)
    ℗ 1983 BMG Music. Courtesy of BMG Ariola Classics GmbH.